# The Lean-Agile Dilemma

## Product Management Inside a Chunky Corporate

**Katie Tamblin**

Apress®

*The Lean-Agile Dilemma: Product Management Inside a Chunky Corporate*

Katie Tamblin
Welwyn, UK

ISBN-13 (pbk): 979-8-8688-0320-8          ISBN-13 (electronic): 979-8-8688-0321-5
https://doi.org/10.1007/979-8-8688-0321-5

Managing Director, Apress Media LLC: Welmoed Spahr
Acquisitions Editor: Shivangi Ramachandran
Development Editor: James Markham
Project Manager: Jessica Vakili

Distributed to the book trade worldwide by Springer Science+Business Media New York, 1 New York Plaza, New York, NY 10004. Phone 1-800-SPRINGER, fax (201) 348-4505, e-mail orders-ny@springer-sbm.com, or visit www.springeronline.com. Apress Media, LLC is a California LLC and the sole member (owner) is Springer Science + Business Media Finance Inc (SSBM Finance Inc). SSBM Finance Inc is a **Delaware** corporation.

For information on translations, please e-mail booktranslations@springernature.com; for reprint, paperback, or audio rights, please e-mail bookpermissions@springernature.com.

Apress titles may be purchased in bulk for academic, corporate, or promotional use. eBook versions and licenses are also available for most titles. For more information, reference our Print and eBook Bulk Sales web page at http://www.apress.com/bulk-sales.

Any source code or other supplementary material referenced by the author in this book is available to readers on GitHub. For more detailed information, please visit https://www.apress.com/gp/services/source-code.

If disposing of this product, please recycle the paper.

# Table of Contents

# About the Author

**Katie Tamblin** started her career as an entry-level analyst and made it all the way to the board room, working as Chief Product Officer and now serving as a Non-Executive Director to data and tech businesses and an Advisor to private equity firms. She applies the learnings amassed over a 25 year career to help readers recognize a chunky corporate for what it is and to navigate its unique qualities in order to drive efficiency and success.

# Introduction

As a product professional, I have spent hundreds of hours writing business cases for new products. I've spent even more time evaluating business cases related to software product development. In retrospect, it seems like a lot of wasted energy because, looking back on it, I can see now what was invisible at the time. Business leaders have very specific conditions under which they will approve a business case or enhancement request. At large, mature tech-enabled businesses, these criteria differ wildly from what the textbooks will tell you. Making sound product decisions and executing a technology transformation efficiently depend on a shared understanding of the objectives of your leadership team—objectives that stretch well beyond the boundaries of what a product can do.

*The Lean-Agile Dilemma* is a compilation of lessons I learned over a 25-year career in data and product management. It is designed to help product managers, engineers, and business leaders work more effectively. I am not speaking from the perspective of a management consultant or academic, but from the experience of an entry-level employee who climbed up the corporate ladder, rung by rung.

I started out as an analyst at Delta Air Lines after finishing university in 2000. After pursuing a master's degree, I was hired at an economic forecasting company as an economist. Over the coming years, across multiple companies, I was promoted to Team Manager, Product Manager, Product Director, Head of Product and Pricing, Chief Product Officer, and Board Member. I managed the supply chain product portfolio for a $5 billion in annual revenue information behemoth called IHS-Markit (now part of S&P Global). I have run product, marketing, technology, and data science teams for private equity-backed technology businesses. I advise a number of private equity houses with combined asset investments of over $220 billion.

I am not the CEO of a software unicorn. You've probably never heard of most of the companies for which I've worked. But I have watched, at every level within an organization, how colleagues at everyday technology-enabled businesses misunderstand, misinterpret, and misapply the things their business leaders want them to do. Senior leaders think their people understand the goals of the business, but that does not mean colleagues know how to align their daily activities to delivering business goals. It is extremely difficult to see from the top where things are going wrong. It is much easier to understand how projects get off track, and how to get them back on track, when you are down in the weeds, making daily decisions that impact the business. I write from that perspective – in the thick of it, rather than the view from the top.

Throughout my career, the more experience I gained working on large technology transformations, the more I felt Lean-Agile wasn't a good fit in my working environment. I was taught (repeatedly) to follow the Lean-Agile method for product and software development. Simultaneously, it was impressed upon me, by the actions of senior leadership, that product and software innovation would not be given room in the corporate budget. I felt like a kid stuck in a custody battle, with one parent espousing one method and another parent regularly undermining it. And, why, I asked myself, was this feeling of push-and-pull constant across multiple companies and roles? Well, it's because it comes from a mismatch between popular development principles and the priorities of an investor-backed business. Let me explain.

*The Lean Startup: How Constant Innovation Creates Radically Successful Businesses* is a phenomenal book whose success created a population of product managers that want to innovate intelligently. Its publication in 2011 marked the beginning of a paradigm shift in Agile culture. It speaks directly to product managers and product owners, who go on to enthusiastically apply Lean-Agile principles wherever they work. When they join the workforces of typical mature organizations, however, they are met with a stark reality check. The bigger the company, the more they struggle to apply Lean-Agile principles.

Agility is not a natural attribute for a group of hundreds or thousands of individuals working alongside each other. Building software and managing data effectively depends on efficient collaboration. However, when you have more people on a project, that gets harder. Lean-Agile principles are meant for small teams innovating radically to identify and capture new markets. The clue is right there in the title: *Constant Innovation*. Investor-owned businesses don't want constant innovation. They want predictable performance. Innovation is risky and unpredictable. Bigger, more established businesses need a different toolkit – one built for what I call "chunky corporates," not lean startups.

This book is part catharsis – I wrote it to process and understand why things go wrong when they go wrong. The how-to portions of this work are derived from many years of screwing up. By learning the hard way how *not* to, and then working out by reflection, trial and error, what might be a better approach, I have found solutions to common challenges. My aim is to help others avoid common mistakes. Over the following chapters, I will outline in detail how software projects get off track. We find a common theme in the misapplication of Lean-Agile principles.

To start, I explain how chunky corporates differ from startups and why that makes Lean-Agile principles a poor fit. Even the giants of Meta, the company formerly known as Twitter, Microsoft, and Google shed thousands of workers in the early 2020s as their investor/owners demanded margin growth. They, too, have become chunky corporates. I'll explain how individual players in the corporate organization impact business performance. We follow the story of Blake, a well-meaning but ultimately naive CEO of a fictional company called Acme Tech (see Figure 1 for a simplified organization chart).

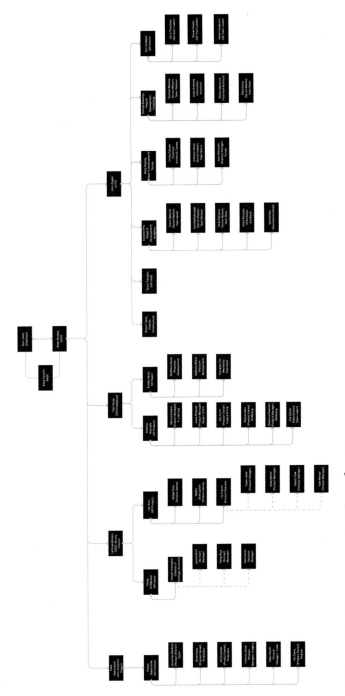

*Figure 1.* Acme organization chart

As Blake and Acme struggle to maintain business performance, I help Blake understand how embedded and complex his challenges are. Effective software development in large organizations depends on efficient communication across large groups operating simultaneously. That is incredibly difficult to achieve. In the thousands of decisions product managers, product owners, data scientists, architects, and engineers make on a daily basis, they determine the future prospects of Acme.

Building software is the easy part. Managing expectations and coordinating activities across a large group of people is hard. I demonstrate how individual motivations, character traits, and skills impact product decisions. When Acme's product decisions are not aligned to the goals of the organization, products undermine business performance, rather than supporting it. This is a very real challenge that nearly all mature software businesses will face.

We see how easily business performance can falter and how difficult it is to get back on track. Throughout the book, Blake and I navigate common issues that erupt when various divisions of his company encounter challenges, like rebuilding aging software, fixing data issues, and product fragmentation. I help Blake to steer Acme back to where it should be: on the path of predictable financial growth sought by its investors. I outline a new software development methodology that takes the best of Lean-Agile but adapts it to the constraints chunky corporates face.

The mistakes, inefficiencies, and failures described in the book are based on real-life experience. The mistakes are my own, and I bear full responsibility for them. They were either errors in my own judgment or in the judgment of a team in which I was an active participant. None of my anecdotes are meant as an indictment of the decisions we made at the time. Most of us are doing the best we can with the resources we have. More than anything, I hope all my battle scars earned on the corporate front lines can help others to start from a stronger foundation. Managing transformational technology projects in a large mature business is inevitable. Delivering them efficiently – to a high standard, on budget, and on time – can be your competitive edge in a fast-moving market. Not doing so could be your downfall.

That being said, as I prepare to share my reflections with the world, I feel I should make a caveat, lest the Internet trolls start doling out judgment of my hypocrisies (of which I have plenty). Early in my career, I sought promotions as validation that I was good at my job. I wanted to win, to succeed, to get to the top because I am goal-oriented and competitive. However, I learned along my journey that getting to the top of the corporate ladder is not the endgame.

There is always another competition, another level of play higher than the current one. The mountain you are climbing has no summit. If you find yourself on a ledge that feels like the top, it is only a matter of time before you find another ledge above you. A bigger role at the same company or the same role at a bigger company functions like a carrot hanging just out of reach, motivating you (as it would a donkey) to just keep walking.

Corporate cultures that use blind ambition to motivate staff are breeding grounds for corporate politics. Politics are a catalyst for inefficiency and an inhibitor to growth. Genuinely, the biggest time-waster in most of my roles was managing political agents working on agendas not aligned to the core aims of the business. Growth is great. Winning is fantastic. But balance is more important in the long run. I love going to work, but I love coming home more. That has kept me sane throughout the weird and not-so-wonderful chapters of several funky projects.

As I matured in my career, I found better ways to pursue sustainable business performance. Letting down personal defenses helps us achieve effective collaboration, which sucks the oxygen out of political agents. We need to change our mindset from zero-sum competition to efficient, collaborative systems for chunky corporates to deliver predictable performance. Every chunky corporate is a system, and if there isn't the right balance in the work system, workers will find the pace of growth unsatisfying and unsustainable. Our common goal is to create work environments that deliver predictable financial performance without sacrificing the health or sanity of our people.

Lean startups might be sexy, but they are scary as well (being a little bit scary is probably what makes them attractive, which is a separate book altogether). However, constant change is not a strong foundation for the mental health of employees. Over time, people want positive and stable environments in which they can work successfully and predictably. Mature, predictable businesses need to see those qualities as desirable. They should stop chasing the lean dream. Chunky corporates have a lot going for them: when managed well, they have the potential to be safe havens in a relentlessly unstable world.

# CHAPTER 1

# The Luxury of a Lean Startup

Imagine yourself in a board-style meeting room, across the table from Blake, the CEO of a successful company, Acme Tech. It's 2 p.m. on a Wednesday afternoon, and Blake wears a pasted-on smile. It's forced. He knows it. You know it. You both pretend all is well. To your right is the Chairman of the Board of Directors for Acme, Don, who was appointed by Acme's private equity (PE) owners. Scattered around the table are business leaders and Board members. The conversation starts off congenially, but the team is not relaxed. Once the pleasantries have completed, Blake hands the presentation over to his Chief Financial Officer (CFO), Luke.

Luke looks uncomfortable. Sales are behind forecast, and costs are up. Luke has a handful of reasons why, logically, this is just a blip. "Sales growth will return next quarter. I am confident," he says, but his body language suggests what we all suspect: the business has lost momentum. It is the same feeling you get when you watch your favorite sports team start to lose a game. You can't explain why; they just aren't playing as a team. They aren't executing on the things they have been trained to deliver. But how can you shift momentum when you don't know the root cause of the downturn in performance? How can Blake get his corporate team back on track?

© Katie Tamblin 2024
K. Tamblin, *The Lean-Agile Dilemma*, https://doi.org/10.1007/979-8-8688-0321-5_1

Luke completes his presentation. The mood has shifted. What started as a congenial conversation closes as a stiff and slightly awkward exchange of generic sentences we all say before parting. The frost in the air reveals a shared concern. Don and the private equity associates leave the room. Blake rubs his temples, visibly agitated.

"We are losing customers," he says, "I'm sure it will turn around. We have really good people. We are customer-driven, and I have been working hard to get the team to be *lean* and *agile*."

I don't believe him, though, and neither does the Board. The momentum has shifted. Startup competitors with more modern products are taking market share. Acme is no longer winning. Blake embarks on a fact-finding mission to understand what is behind the change in financial performance. He puts pressure on his managers to deliver results and get leaner. Despite his emphasis on innovation and customer responsiveness, the behavior he observes at his organization is not *lean* or *agile*. It is quite the opposite. Blake is not leading a lean startup. Blake is the CEO of a chunky corporate: a large, mature organization struggling to apply lean principles effectively. If Blake is going to be successful in turning his business around, he needs a new corporate identity and a new method for unlocking productivity: one that is better matched to the unique properties that define a chunky corporate.

---

**Note**    Lean startup refers to a product development methodology appropriate for new companies or new products. The lean startup method advocates developing products that consumers have demonstrated they will use, proving market existence as the product is launched. The term was coined by Eric Ries, in his incredibly successful and influential book, *The Lean Startup: How Constant Innovation Creates Radically Successful Businesses.*

---

In contrast to a chunky corporate, a lean startup doesn't have a legacy to deliver. It doesn't have hundreds of existing customers that demand an ever-expanding list of products and features. It isn't moving customers from a previous generation platform to a new one. A lean startup has a blank sheet of paper on which to craft a beautiful portrait of a product suite. It may sound counterintuitive, but lean startups have the luxury of time. Most lean startups are not beholden to risk-averse investors. [Most lean startups aren't beholden to investors at all. Only a small portion are lucky enough to raise venture capital (VC) funding, and VC investors are not risk-averse.] Lean startups are not, in the early days, answering to existing customers on a daily basis who remind them of unfixed bugs, features they asked for that haven't been delivered, or additional items they would like to see added to the platform.

The luxury of a lean startup is in its constraints: anonymity, lack of revenue, lack of existing customers, lack of third-party investor/owners, and lack of a predefined product roadmap. A lean startup has the luxury of freedom but the constraint of resources. This keeps teams small, and the roadmap agile. In that context, the principles espoused in Ries's seminal work, *The Lean Startup*, are a fantastic guide for how to develop a new product and ensure there is a market ready for the product when it is built. Applying Ries's principles can, indeed, be the difference between success and failure of a startup.

Attractive startups, like those operating in hot markets – cyber security, blockchain, or supply chain transparency, for example – can be valued at one thousand times their annual revenue and change the world. Most, however, fail to make a dent in the universe or even survive the first few years. It is safe to say the probability of achieving a high valuation on a startup is small. This wide array of possibilities facing any new business, from wild success to abject failure, is what makes a startup glamorous. A startup is the Danny Zuko of the business world: unpredictable and exciting, but also the one your parents warned you about. We should respect those businesses that survive the early years; achieving success at a startup is a hard-fought road.

As a result of these origins, the culture of a successful startup is miles away from the typical culture prevalent at a mature organization with more history. The differences between the two have important implications for how they can unlock sustainable growth. The aim of this analysis is to provide a useful compare-and-contrast between immature and mature organizations in the software industry, enabling all organizations to capture the best of both. An immature organization should aim to be lean. A mature organization must first understand when it is not.

When chunky corporates apply lean principles to product development, it creates tension and frustration rather than radical success. The constraints that chunky corporates face are very different from those that startups face. Before deciding how to solve its product challenges, a business must first be aligned on what it is and what its goals are. A number of chunky corporate constraints result from answering to external investors or shareholders. The cadence of the budgeting and reporting process associated with investor ownership puts a level of scrutiny on revenue coming in the door and costs going out the door that changes the relationship between the organization and its customers. It changes the organization's values. The longer those processes have been in place, the more transformational the change in values.

# Lean-Agile vs. Waterfall Software Development

The Agile software development methodology relies on the collaborative effort of self-organizing and cross-functional teams to deliver and release software frequently to end users. The methodology was popularized by the Manifesto for Agile Software Development[1] and calls for

---

[1] Beck, Kent, James Grenning, Robert C Martin, Mike Beedle, Jim Highsmith, Steve Mellor, Arie van Bennekum, et al. "Agile Software Development." Manifesto for Agile Software Development, 2001. http://agilemanifesto.org/.

adaptive planning, evolutionary development, early delivery, continual improvement, and flexible responses to changes in requirements, capacity, and understanding of the problems to be solved.

Waterfall is a software development methodology introduced in the 1970s that became the dominant method practiced in the 1980s and 1990s. In the Waterfall method of software development, all required features for a platform are defined in advance. Large projects are outlined, mapped out, and then built. Waterfall is the Big Bang of software development. Spend a year (or more) developing a product, release it to the market, and hope your customers like it as much as you do. Developers often work for months without colleagues or customers seeing what they have done. When the work is done according to the definition, the product is shared internally for quality assurance (QA) testing, and shortly thereafter, it will be shared with customers. I say *shortly thereafter* because project leaders assume developers understand the requirements perfectly and the only thing to do in the quality assurance process is to fix bugs, not adjust the underlying functionality. This creates a really funny tension in the post-build world in which teams will argue, often at length, over whether feedback from users constitutes a bug, a design gap, or a new feature. Let me assure you, those conversations are as soul-destroying as they sound.

The Agile methodology came along to disrupt that way of working (and rightly so!). Agile replaced Waterfall as the dominant methodology in the early 2000s. It stresses collaborative iteration that is more responsive to change than Waterfall. Agile popularized the concept of organizing teams in scrums to maximize collaboration and visualizing workflows via Kanban methods. It is highly effective at driving efficiency in the software development, or build, process. By engaging users earlier in the process, you increase visibility, adaptability, and accountability. Lean principles developed alongside the Agile development methodology as it matured.

*The Lean Startup* introduced the concept of a Minimum Viable Product (MVP), in which you develop as little as you possibly can before putting your software product in front of customers. Lean principles help development teams efficiently identify product-market fit. Alongside it, Agile governs the structure and processes of teams as they develop and release code. Lean and Agile are so tightly connected in most software working environments these days; many practitioners of Lean-Agile principles couldn't say with confidence which bits are "Lean" and which bits are "Agile." I will refer to Lean-Agile as the application of Lean principles in the context of Agile software delivery.

Through collaboration and iteration, Lean-Agile limits the inefficiencies associated with misunderstanding the requirements. By "misunderstanding the requirements," I am describing the inevitable situation in which the software engineering team doesn't build exactly what was intended. Whether you are working on Waterfall or Lean-Agile projects, the hardest thing for people to see is what *isn't* there. I know it sounds simple, but the impossible task placed upon product managers and product owners is to identify what you've missed before you hand requirements over to a software engineering team and ask them to build a feature. You only see what you missed when the software is in front of you. At that moment you realize you can't complete your task because a button is missing or a piece of data that you need isn't available. What was built doesn't meet the business need if users can't complete tasks.

By giving users a chance to test early and often, Lean-Agile is more suited to addressing our human proclivity to miss stuff and prevents more software being built on top of an already inadequate feature. This makes the build more efficient because if you build more code on top of a feature that is missing something, you have to add that something back in multiple places (the original feature and anywhere else that depends on that feature). If you catch it early, you aren't left scrambling trying to adjust the rest of the code base to account for this new element. Let me explain.

Imagine a blank sheet of paper. On that sheet of paper, you draw a room. It is a usual square box. It has a door and a window. You show it to your colleague, Nadim, who says, "That is a nice room; it could use some furniture." So, you add some furniture: a sofa and some chairs. The furniture you add suggests it is a living room. You show it to a lovely family, the Joneses, who are planning on building a house. They say, "We could really do with a kitchen." So, you draw a kitchen. This process continues until you have drawn the whole house. In the end, the Joneses want a four-bedroom house with a kitchen, living room, playroom, and home office. You have drawn the whole thing in collaboration with them. Then you give that to a construction company, and they build it. Then the Joneses move in.

Three weeks into the move, the Joneses realize they really should have put a power outlet on the south wall of the living room, not the north wall, because they want to put the television on the south wall, but there is nowhere to plug it in. Then they realize they should have added another room because they really want a home gym. They also wish they had put in one of those integrated vacuum systems, but it is too late now. Within a year, the Joneses are altering the layout of the house, making electrical adjustments, and changing all sorts of things that seemed like a good idea on paper. With a house, you don't really know what you want until you live in it. It is the same with software. The above is a Waterfall method: you draw what you want – thinking you've thought of everything – and then hand it over to be built. Then as soon as you start using it, you find all sorts of other things you wish you had.

If you were to build a house in the Lean-Agile method, the Joneses would move in as soon as the living room was built but before it was decorated. Then they would try out all the locations of where the television might go, and the build team would wire it in appropriately. Then they would add the integrated vacuum system, build a kitchen, then the bedrooms, the home office, the playroom, and the home gym. The Joneses would be constantly feeding to the build team what they want and testing how they will use it before the build is considered complete. And the build team wouldn't move on to another project until the Joneses are happy and settled in their new home.

A lean startup can focus on building the house one room at a time and getting that room right before moving on to the next one. If the Joneses never had a house before, they would likely be willing to go on this journey. A living room on its own still seems like a pretty great offering if your previous experience was living in a tent on a field. But imagine if the Joneses already have a four-bedroom house and you are proposing to move them into a new house. In that case, they aren't likely to move in to a living room on its own. A living room isn't a viable alternative to a family living in a four-bedroom house. Similarly, a customer using a really sophisticated software platform is unlikely to accept a massively slimmed down MVP as a reasonable alternative. This is a serious constraint for companies that need to replatform their product stack. Users are unwilling to try out an MVP when they already have a more robust solution in place.

# What Is Replatforming?

Replatforming is the exercise all mature software businesses will face at some point: having to rebuild the technology that supports their products. In contrast to building a new product with previously non-existing features, *replatforming* refers to the re-building, re-factoring, and/or wholesale replacement of a set of software applications that already exist. When your "new" software build must support existing customers, you are beholden to rebuild old functionality first before you can layer in truly new features. Let's look at the two dominant software methodologies in the context of replatforming.

I worked on a Waterfall project many years ago. The goal was to take a set of spreadsheet calculations and replace them with a web platform. I met with the development team several times before the platform build began. Six months later, I was shown a web platform that was about to be released to our customers. I didn't love it, but it did the job. We released it to our customers. Most were happy. It was definitely smoother and better looking than the spreadsheet they had before. But here's the thing: people interact differently with a software platform than they do with a spreadsheet, so we learned a lot from watching our customers use the new product. They had lots of feedback on what could be better (as did I), but that didn't matter much because by the time it was released, the development team had already moved on to another Waterfall project.

Until real people are using software, you cannot optimize it. It would require an unreasonable amount of abstract thought to anticipate the ways in which a customer will interact with a piece of software until she is actually doing so. The inefficiency of Waterfall is in the assumption that you know what you want to build. The reality is that you never know all of the details up front. Even if you did know, by the time you built it, they will have changed. Lean-Agile processes give you the ability to test the core of the platform and validate your assumptions early. It gives you the ability to pivot if you find that the way people interact with the software is different from how you thought they would. This works really well when you are building a new product: something customers have never seen before. If it is new, customers have no preconceived notions about how it should work, or what it should do. A new product or a new market is the most appropriate place for Lean-Agile development methodology.

A replatforming exercise, though, is inherently half-Waterfall in nature because a version of the software already exists. You already know the range of features you need to deliver. You cannot go to market with an MVP that has fewer features than your customers are using today. Given how large existing feature sets are at chunky corporates, it means that the concept of an MVP doesn't really work for replatforming. That puts replatforming in conflict with the ethos of Lean-Agile development. In one Lean-Agile replatforming project, we compiled a list of the features currently available across all of our existing platforms. There were over a thousand product features in total. We would need to replace these for our customers to migrate them from the old platforms to a new one. This would enable us to decommission the old platforms and make our technology stack more efficient.

The list of features, though, represented over five years' worth of work for twelve development teams, or more than a hundred engineers working concurrently. The sheer amount of functionality the company had built up over its operational history was astounding. Five years of development work to re-build what already existed left us standing still in the market.

We had little or no capacity to add new features or products and test them. We were handcuffed to a roadmap predefined by the customer upgrade schedule. We called it an "Agile" project, but it was more akin to Waterfall development than Agile.

One hundred percent of development capacity was spent on rebuilding existing features, and we did not have the freedom to respond to change. The only value-add open to us was to build features in a new way that made them more modern and better able to stand the test of time. You can reimagine the old stuff, but it still has to achieve the business outcome of the previous product. This, to a large degree, acts like a ball and chain to your product roadmap. When you work at a chunky corporate, eighty percent to ninety-five percent of the time you are focused on making better what the company already built. The longer your company has been operating and building software, the more you'll have to rebuild or replace. Equally, the more fragmented your existing product stack, and organization, the longer it will take and the harder it will be.

# Product Fragmentation

Fragmentation refers to the level to which a product stack has, or, more precisely, doesn't have, a strong technical backbone of consistency built around a common value proposition. In a fragmented product stack, there are different software products with overlapping features and random product features that don't fit neatly into the technology stack or product value proposition. High levels of product fragmentation require replatforming. As products fragment, their product stacks diverge. Divergence leads to replication, which is inefficient to maintain. A fragmented product stack is like a disorganized closet. There are lots of little boxes with random contents without any overarching logic behind which contents are in which box. Like the closet, a fragmented product stack has disorganized, random, and overlapping features. Fragmentation can be a result of mismanagement of Lean-Agile development, acquisitions, or federated growth.

Lean-Agile principles encourage us to regularly release new features to determine if demand exists. If demand does not exist, we pivot and discontinue the unadopted features. However, in a fragmented product stack, a number of features survive in a constant state of low, but not zero, usage. Often this is a result of being a little too customer-led. A customer requests a feature; we add it, and only that customer uses it. If we constantly deliver new features without managing end-of-life for the less successful ones, the platform will, over time, have a long tail of barely used features.

Misapplication of Lean-Agile product innovation results in features that don't fit the core value proposition. If we were truly following Lean-Agile principles, we would decommission, or sunset, these features when we find they are not supportive of the core value proposition. Underutilized features should be deprecated, the practice in which users are advised not to use a feature in preparation for its decommissioning. It is harder to deprecate features that vocal customers use, even if we know not enough customers are using them to warrant their maintenance. When we don't have strong enough customer relationships to facilitate a confident, positive conversation about features set for decommissioning, it is easier to ignore the problem and just leave the features in place.

Let's look at an example of fragmentation arising from acquisitive growth. Here we have a company acquiring another company to gain synergies in the product line and the customer base. Acme Tech's Analytics Division sells analytical reports in London covering markets in Europe. Acme decides to acquire FinUSA, a company selling financial reports that covers markets in the United States. FinUSA was founded ten years ago by a woman named Stephanie. With the acquisition, Acme can now sell European reports to American customers and US reports to European customers.

Acme benefits from a single sales and marketing infrastructure that can sell both types of reports. Over time, the analysts writing the reports find that they are both publishing some generic content at the start of every report (whether US or European) outlining global market conditions. When these reports came from two separate companies, there were different teams writing this content. Now they are both owned by Acme; there are two teams doing the same thing. At a minimum, this is inefficient. It really gets awkward when the two analytics teams do not come to the same conclusion about global market conditions. In all likelihood, it will be a customer that first asks the question: "So, I bought the US and European reports, and the US report says the global economy will grow by two percent next year, but the European report says the global economy will grow by two and a half percent next year. Why is that? And which figure should I trust?"

The reason I say it will likely be a customer that points this out before the company does anything about it is because that has been my first-hand experience. It is a logical outcome. Firstly, the alignment of sales and marketing resources typically happens faster than the alignment of product resources. Blake and Don are focused on the revenue synergies (as in, sell the US reports in Europe) more than they are concerned with what is in the reports. So, the analysts writing the reports are left on their own to keep writing the reports as they are. Many analysts are not immediately informed that there is overlapping content with the European reports, so both teams just keep doing what they do, leaving everyone none the wiser.

This, in my experience, is the most likely scenario for the first six to twelve months post-acquisition. Eventually, the analysts realize there is another team in Acme putting out conflicting analysis of global market conditions, but both teams believe their analysis is the most accurate and therefore are reluctant to change. This is typically how the team will operate from twelve to twenty-four months post-acquisition. From this point forward, we have the possibility of conflict. Both teams that author the global content will be worried they may lose their jobs if the other team wins the battle. So each team has an incentive to make the case as to why their global content is either better, or at a minimum, different, from the other. If both teams are successful at arguing the case for differentiation, they both remain, leaving inefficiency in the business, and allowing for two divergent teams to do the same thing in different ways. This is fragmentation: multiple products deliver the same business outcome without logical distinction.

Rather than a common backbone of product (a single global section used in multiple reports), you start to have duplication and incentives to create differentiation where it is not necessary. In reading this, you may think to yourself: "Surely that never happens. A strong leadership team would spot the inefficiency of duplication and prevent this." That is certainly true in theory. One of the biggest issues in a chunky corporate is that practice does not line up with theory. In reality, leadership teams miss things. Few business leaders or investors in the business to business (B2B) space actually use the products they sell. Blake and Don don't read the detailed US and EU market reports their company sells. They haven't noticed this issue directly. Equally, Blake could get talked into leaving inefficiency in the business by the stakeholders who benefit from it: in this case, the team leaders of the analysts writing about global financial conditions. These team leaders are under increased stress due to the instability introduced by Acme's acquisition.

Merger and acquisition activity is some of the most stress-inducing work I have experienced. I have talked to countless founders who have experienced all sorts of physiological maladies as a result of the stress that comes with sale or equity raising processes for their businesses: back pain, ulcers, severe cases of anxiety, or, at a minimum, general grumpiness. Selling a business is the culmination of years' worth of blood, sweat, and tears. The thorough examination of a business that accompanies a sale process can be exhausting. Investors look for evidence of performance across all key elements of the business. Finance, sales, product, and technology can all expect to be cross-examined in a manner more befitting a witness in a murder case than your typical conference room chat. If you survive it, it can make or break your career prospects in the new business.

When the dust settles on an acquisition, the hard work begins. Companies are acquired by larger businesses because they are one of three things to the acquiring organization: a competitor, the owner of a complementary offering, or a disruptor in the acquiring incumbent's core market. The founder or owner of a company is, by the nature of how a company ends up for sale, supportive of the idea of being acquired. There are financial gains to be had, and typically a sale scratches the competitive itch of a founder by validating that she has created value in her business. However, just because the founder is on board with the acquisition goal, it doesn't mean all of her colleagues are on board with the idea.

Due to the confidential nature of acquisitions, most employees at the organization being acquired are informed when the sale happens. They turn up to work one day and find themselves flung into a new reality: one in which they may no longer be confident of how they fit within the organization. Decisions will no longer be made by the colleagues they know; the new company leaders may not understand their value or their roles.

Unless you have an uncharacteristically healthy level of confidence, this can be a scary prospect. *What if all that I offer isn't obvious to the new leadership team? What if there is someone at the new organization who does my job better than I do? What if the company decides that my role isn't important anymore? Where will that leave me?* These fears can create some pretty gnarly incentives across the organization. If colleagues feeling unsettled by an acquisition are nervous about their future roles, they have an incentive to build up defenses that will secure their individual futures. Those defenses can often run counter to the efficiency of the business.

Stephanie was thrilled to sell FinUSA to Acme, for example. She announces with pride to her team of 200 employees that the company has been sold. Blake and his leadership team spend the next several weeks traveling to Stephanie's offices across the United States and getting to know their new colleagues. Jonathan is a Product Director in Stephanie's company and has worked for Stephanie for all ten years since she started the company. Jonathan's product portfolio includes the web platform via which the US financial reports are delivered. When the new leadership team arrives at Jonathan's office, he is nervous. He has been invited to meet Blake.

Jonathan can't help but feel he is about to interview for his existing job. He worries Blake won't like him. He worries there is someone already at Acme who could manage the analyst team across both companies, and he will lose his job. Jonathan has every incentive to spend his hour with Blake explaining why the US reports are unique. Jonathan is justifying his own existence. It doesn't really matter if the products are truly different or not. Jonathan instinctively believes, for his own survival, it is important Blake *thinks* his products are different. If everyone acts like Jonathan, Blake will not get a very honest appraisal of Stephanie's company or the products they make and sell. If Jonathan is successful, Blake will not push to integrate products across the two organizations. Not integrating products keeps Jonathan in a place where he is comfortable and confident in his role and secures his future.

Wasn't the point of acquiring Stephanie's company to drive efficiency, though? What if the US and European software products are actually quite similar? If the products could be combined into a single software platform providing global reports with regional detail, it will require fewer developers to maintain them going forward. Both products can benefit from a single roadmap of new software features. That would make for happier customers (because both US and European customers benefit from enriched features), better margins (as Acme can support both products with less resources), and a more efficient business.

How is Blake to know the right way forward? Will he recognize that listening to Jonathan will introduce fragmentation to his product stack? Blake will have to form his own view because Jonathan's actions are too influenced by his desire to secure his own future. Will Blake have the time and headspace to check that what Jonathan tells him is accurate? Once a decision is made, company leaders will have to manage the teams carefully to ensure the decision is implemented. Blake may say he wants the products integrated, but it will be Jonathan and his East Coast counterpart that lead the software integration. They will have many opportunities to block or manipulate Blake's intentions if they are motivated by self-preservation above product efficiency.

Federated organic growth in a business can also fragment a product stack over time. Fragmentation in this context arises from the instinct to focus on how customers in a particular cohort (like a region, or a specific industry) are different from other customers, rather than focusing on how they are similar. Acme's Survey Division has a regional leader, Johannes, who manages the Survey business in Germany. Johannes knows the German customers better than anyone and has been responsible for significant growth in the region. He is acutely aware, and regularly reminded by his customers, that Germany is a unique market with specific requirements. Johannes has worked with the product team to modify the product to reflect Germany's unique characteristics, and it is helping to sell the product well in that region. All of this is positive for the company.

Fast forward ten years. Four other regional leaders have been following in Johannes's footsteps around the world. The company has expanded its markets, and each expansion has required a new copy of the software platform, tailored to the unique requirements of each geography. The company has reached a strong annual turnover, but now the focus is on cost. Maintaining five different regional versions of the web platform is costly. Regional leaders are starting to suspect consolidation is on the horizon.

Here we find ourselves in a prisoner's dilemma of sorts. Individually, each Regional Director has an incentive to preserve the unique characteristics of his regional variation. If he doesn't do this, he could find himself consolidated out of a job. So, each Regional Director has an incentive to build a case to justify his existence and the existence of a regionalized version of the product that brought the region success. Those who fear being consolidated shift into preservation mode, regularly making a case for differentiation and making it very difficult for internal resources to achieve efficiency. Over time, these regional paths continue to develop independently of each other, and, in mature organizations, they take on lives of their own. Without brutal focus on efficiency, over time, this quite commonly results in a fragmented product stack. I worked for one organization with twenty-seven different software platforms that all did roughly the same thing. Twenty-seven! Each had catered to some sort of regional or industry differential that justified its creation and preservation.

## Addressing Product Fragmentation

Over time, fragmentation, whether achieved through misapplication of Lean-Agile principles, federated growth, or acquisition, results in product features that are all over the place. Here are some handy ways to identify fragmentation in your product stack:

1. **Features don't fit neatly into the marketing literature.** If you have a feature, or a set of features, that you struggle to describe in your marketing literature, it is worth asking yourself: Why do they exist? If they are out of alignment with your core value proposition, you should question why you sell them. If you don't have a good reason, make a plan to divest or sunset these features.

2. **Features are only used by one or a small number of customers.** Saying yes to your customers is great when their wants are aligned to your business's growth engine, but saying yes to your customers when they want features that no one else in your target audience will use can be margin diluting.

3. **Features are broken across legacy business lines.**
   This is often the result of regional- or industry-based
   separation of products or acquisitions that results in
   duplication. In these cases, it is important to pursue
   objective and thorough evaluation of product
   differentiation. Multiple product lines and features
   should be, at a minimum, served by a common
   backbone of technology infrastructure wherever
   possible, and, at best, integrated, where appropriate.

Product fragmentation is not always preventable. When it is
recognized, it should be addressed, which usually requires replatforming.
Various products and features across the fragmented product stack require
new infrastructure and new software applications that strategically reduce
fragmentation and drive efficiency in the stack. This is one of the main
reasons replatforming projects recur at relatively regular intervals for
mature businesses seeking perpetual growth. We will discuss this in detail
in Chapter 7.

# Key Takeaways

- Lean-Agile principles are meant for small teams
  radically innovating to identify new product markets.

- Replatforming is the method by which chunky
  corporates rebuild outdated or unfit software.

- Product fragmentation describes software products
  suffering from duplication and underutilized features.

- Replatforming is usually required to correct a
  fragmented product stack.

# CHAPTER 2

# Execution, Not Innovation

The difference between execution and innovation is a fundamental point separating chunky corporates from lean startups. Many overlook this difference in their desire to apply Lean-Agile principles at chunky corporates. A startup has the freedom to innovate and follow where growth takes it. A chunky corporate must remain focused on execution in order to preserve what makes it an attractive business: predictability. Innovation is not predictable. Risk dilutes chunky corporate margins in the short term. Investors seek dependable returns over relatively short time horizons and are allergic to diluted margins. As a result of these factors, accepting external investment inevitably adjusts business goals away from innovation and toward reliability. However, most colleagues working at investor-owned businesses seem to miss this point.

© Katie Tamblin 2024
K. Tamblin, *The Lean-Agile Dilemma*, https://doi.org/10.1007/979-8-8688-0321-5_2

**Note**   Eric Ries states, in *The Lean Startup*:[1]

"To open up a new business that is an exact clone of an existing business all the way down to the business model, pricing, target customer, and product may be an attractive economic investment, but it is not a startup because its success depends only on execution – so much so that this success can be modeled with high accuracy."

Business colleagues are wooed by the glamorous life of *The Lean Startup* experience. They hear how amazing it was when a company started out as two people in a garage with an idea. The next thing you know they're on the cover of *GQ* or *Forbes* as a billionaire success story. We've seen *The Social Network* and read *How Google Works*. The success story focuses on super smart individuals in the right place at the right time who effectively applied Lean-Agile principles to the creation of new software products. These sexy stories show how the road may be a bit hard at times, but, in the end, it was all worth it because the new products disrupted the market and were wildly successful. That's a fantastic story; I'd watch that film (I have watched that film). But, as with most glittery stories, they are the exception. The typical reality is much more mundane. Your average product manager would describe her life to be more like a scene from *Office Space*, the 1999 cult comedy classic, than *The Social Network*. Most product managers work at chunky corporates, not lean startups.

A subtle but significant business challenge reflects that many chunky corporate product managers have read *The Lean Startup* and expect a sprinting pace of change as large teams of developers make real their visions for products. When they accept a position at a large, mature organization, they are burdened by reality: a very slow pace, layers of

[1] Ries, Eric. *The Lean Startup: How Constant Innovation Creates Radically Successful Businesses*. Penguin Random House UK, 2011.

documentation, process manuals that span hundreds of pages, and endless sets of approval processes before things move into sprint. This feels epically slow, but this is the reality of product development at mature, successful businesses.

Product managers often think there must be something wrong. *This is not what I signed up for.* In reality, the things that make a chunky corporate successful are not the same things that make a lean startup successful. The biggest challenge for a chunky corporate is staying focused, not innovating. Chunky corporates spend more time reining in the desire to innovate among colleagues with big ideas than they do pursuing new, risky product adventures. Advice on managing a product team should work like a car manual: you have to enter the make and model first before you can download the appropriate instructions. Information in the owner's manual on how to refuel your car, for example, will look quite different for a 1967 Ford Mustang as compared to a 2020 Nissan Leaf.

How you work in a lean startup should look very different from how you work in a chunky corporate, and step one is making sure all of your colleagues recognize what you are and what you are not. This is a key element of having a positive and stable corporate culture. Without a shared identity, there is a risk that corporate culture will fracture across teams. Colleagues need to know what type of organization they work for and how that organization intends to reach its goals. If you are a chunky corporate, embrace being a chunky corporate – they have a lot going for them! Chunky corporates have stable income and deep resources that enable them to plan effectively for the future. Let's not be so hasty as to discount the importance of feeling confident that your business has a future. Lean startups do not often have that luxury.

If you are a chunky corporate, be clear with your entire organization that predictable performance is more important than innovation and disruption. Be straightforward about how resources and investment decisions will be made. This will set appropriate expectations for your team members and help managers across your business set appropriate expectations for colleagues. It will reduce the amount of time wasted building business cases for products the company has no intention of building. Experts say the first step in achieving positive mental health is understanding who you are. Being self-aware as an organization is equally as important. If the understanding of your organization is inappropriate, as in your colleagues think you are a lean startup seeking innovation but in reality you are a chunky corporate seeking predictable growth, you will struggle to pursue common goals effectively.

When your corporate identity is vague, you will have some colleagues chasing new exciting product builds and others pursuing disciplined execution. These differing goals and modes of working will inevitably cause friction. Friction can lead to fracturing, and fracturing breeds inefficiency. If different teams attempt to achieve financial goals in opposing ways, they are more likely to duplicate efforts and cause confusion for the rest of the organization. In short, recognizing you are a chunky corporate enables colleagues across your organization to align their expectations with your reality. If they think they are at a lean startup, they will inevitably be disappointed when reality does not match their expectation.

# Predictable Performance

Let me be clear, when I say predictable performance is more important than innovation, I mean in the context of new product development as described in *The Lean Startup*. I don't mean to imply there should be no innovation across the company. On the contrary, you want colleagues across the business to innovate. However, innovations should have defined boundaries. Innovation in software development should be encouraged and focused on how product features are delivered and built, not what they do. Chunky corporates benefit from innovation related to improvement and maintenance of existing products that have a proven return.

Risky new products could be built to drive growth in new markets. That is always true. However, on the whole, it is simply not in a chunky corporate's interest to use its vast resources to invest in organic growth in new markets. Chasing new markets carries great risk. Chunky corporates will, instead, focus on proven markets as they pursue growth. Chunky corporates may build competitive software, delivering a better version of what competitors already offer. Or they may enter new markets through acquisition, purchasing a lean startup that has proven it can deliver strong growth in what was a previously unproven market. This approach to new markets is something that should be clear for chunky corporate colleagues across the organization.

If colleagues recognize this, they can stay focused on delivering predictable performance in an existing product suite. That is not to say that existing products cannot benefit from enhancements and new features. Certainly they can, but when new features or new products are accompanied by wildly optimistic expectations for the incremental revenue they will drive, the hairs on the back of my neck tend to stand up. Nine times out of ten, those revenue predictions are overestimated. Overestimated revenue generation of unproven products quickly diverts attention from maintaining the success of the existing product stack, as colleagues get excited about pushing the shiny new thing. The aim of staying focused is not to stifle innovation but rather to channel innovation into delivering better versions of the existing product stack to serve proven markets. Innovation can help customers solve problems in new, more efficient ways. To be effective in this way, though, requires a deep understanding of the problems your customers are trying to solve and dedication to serve the existing market.

The role of a product function is to identify the business requirements that balance the needs of many internal and external stakeholders. The greatest contribution of a well-run product team is to deliver success via a scalable and flexible product stack. The discipline required to constantly deliver for existing stakeholders leaves virtually no capacity available for innovation-related trial and error. An exception can sometimes be found when a leadership team sets aside a ring-fenced set of resources dedicated to new product incubation and innovation. In practice, however, at most chunky corporates, these teams either conflict or duplicate efforts with mainstream product teams. Quite frankly, they are the first ones leadership teams eliminate when cost comes under the microscope. Lacking a revenue stream directly associated with your department leaves you exposed to constant risk that your department will be cut. To be a disruptor, or respond quickly to disruptors, resources must be dedicated to innovation in the business. However, if the organization has ever gone through a cost-cutting exercise, as nearly all chunky corporates have, the resources experimenting with risky innovations have already been cut.

One of the most common ways in which mainstream product roadmaps get clogged up with risky development is when colleagues inadvertently step out of their swim lanes and demand new products. Let me explain. Melanie is the VP of Operations in Acme's Publishing Division. Publishing has a strong e-commerce footprint operating in the UK. The Publishing Division sells online academic courses, and Melanie is responsible for ensuring the textbooks that accompany online courses are shipped to students before the courses begin.

Melanie's boss, Tilen, encourages her to find more efficient ways to drive company performance. Melanie suggests that the expansion of its e-commerce site to cover Europe would automate her work processes and open up new markets. Melanie explains that when someone who is based outside of the UK signs up for a course, she has to take payment, print shipping labels, and pay postage manually. She suggests the expansion of Publishing Division's e-commerce site to cover Europe would automate her work processes and open up new markets. Only one percent of students are based outside of the UK, but that still represents hundreds of shipping labels a year. Tilen encourages her to share this idea with the product team.

The product manager for e-learning, Mina, evaluates the opportunity. She loves the idea of going after a new, more international market while improving operational efficiency. She believes the company could double its course bookings by expanding the e-commerce site to take payments in euros. She prepares a business case for Tilen to present to the Board. The Board is skeptical. At only one percent of current bookings, there is no proof consumers in the Eurozone will subscribe to English-speaking courses at a volume that will justify the investment.

Equally, Don, the Board Chairman, has worked on international e-commerce projects before. He knows what Mina does not: software that can support multiple currencies and comply with tax requirements for different countries across the Eurozone is complicated. It will require a large upfront investment in third-party billing technology and a diversion of internal development resources to support the integration of that technology. The Board concludes that the upfront investment to expand the e-commerce site would dilute its margin with no guarantee of future results. They refuse the business case.

A great deal of time and effort could have been saved if Mina and Melanie knew from the outset that chasing new markets is not how the company intends to achieve its goals. Melanie works in operations. When Tilen asked her to innovate, he meant within the realm of operations. However, Melanie's pitch somehow turned into a new software product idea – one that requires upfront investment. Tilen, if he understands the priorities of a chunky corporate, should be able to gently explain to Melanie that large investments in risky software expansions are unlikely to be aligned to the company's strategy. They could brainstorm, however, how they can achieve what Melanie wants to achieve without diluting margins.

Tilen: "Thanks for the presentation, Mina and Melanie. I know you want to take this business case to the Board, but I see two issues here that we need to address. Firstly, we don't have a good commercial grasp on what the online courses market looks like in the Eurozone. Just because we build an international e-commerce site, that doesn't mean the customers will come. Secondly, I want to take a step back and look at what you are trying to achieve, Melanie. I think we got off track here."

Melanie: "My goal here is to not have to spend several working days a year manually printing off shipping labels for our European customers."

Tilen: "You mentioned that you have to take payment manually, too. Is that still an issue?"

Melanie: "I hear that is an issue, but technically it is the finance department that has to take the payment, not me. So, I guess whether or not that is a pain point for the finance team needs validation."

Tilen: "Let's focus on the problem you have first. I am confident there are other ways to solve the issue of postage. I'm not sure it requires a large investment in e-commerce expansion. Let's pull together a workshop to brainstorm that. Surely there is a low-fi solution here, like requiring the small portion of international students that buy from us to go separately to an established bookseller, or even Amazon. If we just discount their course fee and sell the books separately, that could work, right? That gives us an opportunity to solve your problem, Melanie, without taking on the expense of expanding the e-commerce platform."

Melanie: "Maybe. I'll do some research and pull stakeholders together for a workshop to look at alternatives. To be honest, I didn't realize expanding e-commerce into other countries would be a big deal."

Tilen: "Yep, for sure – I get it. I just don't want to distract the technology team with this as they have an already full roadmap. If we can't find an alternative solution to your problem, let me know. Now, on to point two. Mina, I appreciate you've pulled numbers together based on market sizes in the Eurozone. How did we get from solving an operational problem to launching our products into a new market?"

Mina: "Melanie asked us to expand the e-commerce platform. It felt like a win-win because if we did that, we could sell in those markets more effectively."

Tilen: "How do we know there is demand in those markets for our products, though? How would we capture that demand? Would it require investing in a sales team on the Continent? What other players are operating in this market? Would we be better off purchasing a company that is established in Europe? I can't see a build-versus-buy analysis here. The only option presented is for us to build. We have let the proposed solution to Melanie's problem, an e-commerce site, become a motivating factor in making a substantial change in our product strategy. The tail is in danger of wagging the dog, here.

"To pursue these markets effectively would require an expansion of marketing and sales resources as well as technology. Products don't sell themselves. I can't see Blake or the Board going for it, if I am honest. It is too risky. I'm glad to see you both putting ideas forward. I like the mindset. However, we need to stay laser-focused on delivering the business plan. Something big and risky, like expanding the e-commerce site, will divert attention. The probability it helps performance is not any higher than the probability it hurts performance by raising technology costs without a proven return."

In the above scenario, Tilen encourages his team to stay focused on the problem at hand: automating Melanie's operational workflow. He guides Mina in a direction more aligned to business goals. He encourages Melanie and Mina to continue putting ideas forward. The aim here is not to stifle new ideas. However, Tilen needs to keep his team focused and prevent disappointment. Mina would be more annoyed if she submitted a business case to Tilen but never received feedback at all as to why it was ignored. Corrective feedback is better than no feedback. Corrective feedback is a learning opportunity. Mina needs to understand that her job is to focus on execution of the plan, not new product innovation.

# Stay Predictable

We've seen how colleagues across a chunky corporate can inadvertently become demanding customers of new software features. Indeed, Melanie had no idea that to organically expand Publishing Division's e-commerce site, the software team would need to build a host of new features and buy a load of expensive tech. Mina thinks that being the mastermind of a new product that can generate new revenue will be her path to a promotion. Mina struggled to stick to predictable execution of proven features.

Indeed, the lure of shiny new products is strong. However, successfully managing a technology-enabled product stack at a chunky corporate is based in discipline. Product management is about balancing needs. A salesperson needs a new feature to close a deal. A customer success colleague needs an enhancement to keep an existing customer happy. The Board wants predictable revenue and profitability growth. The finance team wants online billing. The operations team wants automated shipping notifications.

All of these competing needs create large demand for software features. In economics, the term Pareto efficiency refers to a distribution of wealth or outcomes in which any other distribution would leave one or more individuals worse off. A Pareto optimal solution, therefore, means the benefit of outcomes is optimized. Whether or not the product management function is serving its intended purpose depends on how well it delivers Pareto optimal solutions to users while keeping revenue growth and cost in line with budget expectations. This is harder than it sounds and also more boring. Product managers must balance voices competing for space on the product roadmap. The voices can be loud. The voices often drown out, or wholly replace, what user behavior tells you.

Lean-Agile principles are built on a foundation of user input. That input can be gathered a number of ways. The most common is platform usage. You can understand how users interact with your platform by spending time with them directly, by tracking what they do when they visit the platform (called usage statistics), or a combination of both.

Another popular method is A/B or split testing, in which case you build two versions of the same feature, A and B, then release version A to some customers and version B to other customers. This mimics scientific experimentation in providing easily comparable results of user interaction with different versions of the same feature. Another glamorous-sounding way to prove market demand for a new feature is through fake-door or trap-door analysis. This is a method whereby you build a fake button on your website to see how many users try to click. It is a good way to validate demand for a new feature you are thinking about building.

There is no shortage of ways in which creative product managers can validate and verify market demand for new products and features. But do most product teams in chunky corporates allow for this? No. In fact, most chunky corporates do not prioritize developing detailed usage statistics, A/B testing, or trap-door techniques because their teams do not have the time or resources to respond to the input these techniques would provide. The product roadmap at chunky corporates is already so overstuffed with planned development that letting customer behavior guide what features go on your roadmap is an unattainable goal. In fact, most roadmaps are already defined for a minimum of twelve to thirty-six months. Even with the plethora of customer behavior monitoring tools available today from low-cost, simple-to-deploy third-party products, they are often not high priority. Why? Because most product managers would not be able to act on the insights usage statistics provide. Most roadmaps at chunky corporates are already defined for the foreseeable future.

The hard work at a chunky corporate comes before Lean-Agile principles can be applied – deciding where to focus when you have more existing products, ideas for enhancements, and customer requests than you have resources to deliver and maintain them. The scope of change is greater than the development capacity available to deliver it. Therefore, directing focus is how product teams add value to the business. These decisions need to be made by product managers and owners who have incredibly sound judgment.

Inevitably, for Acme Tech, there will be more demands for software enhancements than there are resources to serve them. Before the product team gets to the point where it could release and test an MVP, or iterate features based on cool techniques like A/B testing or trap-door analysis, this team first has to get Board approval to invest in development resources, and then needs to decide how to deploy those resources. To secure approval from the Board, the team has already decided *what they are going to build.* Governing boards are rather loath to approve funding for vague tech projects without clear direction or focus. A strong business case requires detail around what features will be built and how much it will cost. That is fundamentally at odds with the Lean-Agile principle of start small and let customer demand dictate where you spend development resources.

Rarely in my product career have I seen a chunky corporate product team with enough development resources to successfully build two versions of a feature and use A-B testing to see which one customers use more. The much more common reality is that product managers work really hard just to get a single, slimmed-down version of the feature customers have been screaming about for the last few years onto the corporate product roadmap. When that feature is finally delivered, it is met with deflated disappointment, either because it was delivered much later than expected, or because the functionality it delivers is less than what was requested.

In the startup world, product managers spend most of their time designing new features to test. At a startup, the people acting as product managers and product owners are also probably the people that founded the business. Startup founders are working on cultivating an orchard by planting a few apple seeds and watching them grow. It takes a great deal of upfront design to get the orchard established. At a large, mature organization, product managers and product owners are tending an existing orchard that was planted years ago, rather than planting for the first time. There isn't much room on the existing plot for more trees.

When tending a mature orchard, the focus is on keeping the trees expertly trimmed and harvesting fruit at predictable intervals. Product managers at a chunky corporate should spend the majority of time maintaining the orchard, not planting new trees.

Product managers should listen well and proactively communicate back to colleagues and customers what will be developed, what will not be developed, and, most importantly, why. In my experience, communication of the *why* goes a long way to bring colleagues and customers on the development journey with the organization. Customers and colleagues are much more understanding of a feature being delayed or not being developed at all when they are aware of the context.

If they know what features *are* getting developed, they can better understand why the ones they asked for are *not* being developed as a matter of priority. The ideal product manager has a really dynamic mix of skills: enough technical knowledge to know (at a high level) what software and data can or cannot do, enough research and analytical skills to gather the required information and make good decisions, and enough people skills to take colleagues and customers with them on the journey of platform development. Table 2-1 lists the importance of each skill.

***Table 2-1.*** *Variations in importance of product manager skills based on the corporate context*

| Product Manager Skills | Chunky Corporate | Lean Startup |
| --- | --- | --- |
| Listening | Very important | Important |
| Communicating | Very important | Less Important |
| Influencing | Very important | Less Important |
| Design | Less Important | Very important |
| Analytical | Important | Very important |
| Risk-taking | Less Important | Very important |

Product managers must develop a deep understanding of customer (both internal and external) needs and confidently determine the priority order of various features for development. Once the priorities are agreed, they can be divided up among the relevant product owners. It is then the job of product managers to accurately hand over that deep understanding of the desired outcomes of each feature to the product owner. When product owners understand the context of the features, including the desired outcomes customers want to achieve, they are in the best possible position to document requirements focused on outcomes.

One major challenge in the product management space is that most product managers don't get into product management to spend their time talking to people. They get into product management to design products. However, at a chunky corporate, that is a very small part of the job. The much more important and much more time-consuming part of the job is figuring out what products or features should be built – not how they should work or look. This decision-making process is not nearly as satisfying, glamorous, or sexy as product design. It takes time, requires loads of research, and lots of coordination of people across the business and customer base. It can be frustrating because the more people a product manager speaks to, the more likely she is to hear conflicting demands.

Conflicting demands make it difficult to determine the *right* features to build. Determining the right features to build, and perhaps more importantly, what features should not be built, is the greatest value-add a product manager brings to a chunky corporate. Good product managers are data-driven and decisive but not stubborn. They make recommendations to the business based on analysis of data but are confident enough to change those recommendations should more robust data be presented in a counter-argument. Once priorities are agreed, product managers should spend the majority of their time keeping stakeholders aligned and focused on delivering the plan.

At a chunky corporate, product managers should spend less than twenty percent of their time on the design of new features and seventy-five percent of their time talking to people. Of that seventy-five percent of the time talking to people, at least a third of it (twenty-five percent of the total) should be spent out of the office with customers and prospective customers. The other two-thirds (fifty percent of the total) should be spent with colleagues. Product owners, in contrast to product managers, should spend about thirty percent of their time documenting requirements and gathering technical artifacts associated with those requirements (like information architecture design and technical design). Another fifty percent of their time should be spent gathering the appropriate specialists together into squads.

A squad is a team of relevant stakeholders. Similar to Agile methodology, which relies on scrums, or groups of self-organizing engineers working on discrete features, a *squad* is a slightly larger group of players, composed not only of engineers but also subject matter experts and business partners. The squad is responsible for managing solution design appropriately, ensuring what is passed to the development team is understood accurately and developed efficiently, delivering the desired outcome. The scrum is a subset of the squad, responsible for writing code and delivering working software.

If an engineering team is delivering a piece of software that serves operations within the business – like customer relationship management, operational workflows, finance, marketing, or human resources (HR) – a product owner can independently lead and be accountable for ensuring technology services the business need. A product manager is less necessary in these work streams because product managers tend to be outward-facing. When an engineering team is delivering product that is customer-facing, it is more likely that a product owner and a product manager will both be needed. The product manager works closely with the product owner on the commercial need, customer need, and methods for monetizing these needs. The product owner translates these needs into technical requirements. However, for these ways of working to be effective, product managers and product owners need to have strong communication, analytical, and technical skills. Table 2-2 demonstrates an average breakdown of time spent by job function.

***Table 2-2.*** *A realistic allocation of time for product managers and product owners at a chunky corporate[i]*

|  | **Product Manager** | **Product Owner** |
| --- | --- | --- |
| Time with external customers | 25% | <5% |
| Time on product design | <5% | <10% |
| Time with colleagues | 50% | 50% |
| Requirements and delivery | <10% | 30% |

[i]*Yes, I know the figures in this table don't add up to 100%. That would be absurd. If 100% of your time is allocated, when do you go to the bathroom?*

Product owners should have more technical skills than product managers; however, it is equally important that product owners have strong communication skills. They need to be dynamic enough to translate how the tech works into laypersons' terms and explain how the software is going to work and what it will and won't be able to do. Product owners need the people skills to align technical documentation and design with the business requirements and the technical skills to critically review designs and ensure software delivers the desired business outcomes.

They must be obsessed with delivery of working technology that serves a business need. Product owners are accountable to the business in ensuring that released software achieves its desired outcomes and a product owner should not rest nor move on to a new milestone until the product is achieving its stated outcomes (that means no critical bugs, blockers, or showstoppers). Engineers can call a feature done when acceptance criteria are met. Product owners aren't done until the business is happy.

Equally, product owners are responsible for balancing scope creep against business objectives. Making the business happy can mean many different things. It may make individual business stakeholders happy if you add a bunch of features to a milestone based on their feedback in UAT. However, it will not make business leaders happy that you spent $200,000 worth of engineering resources and delivered your milestone three months late because some of the business stakeholders wanted the product to cater for rendering Japanese language characters when less than two percent of the customer base is based in Japan and all of them read English. Product owners need to balance the needs of all business stakeholders and manage the conflict between them. This takes a mix of analytical and people skills.

What is altogether too common, though, is product managers and owners are either strong in an analytical skill-set or strong in a people skill-set but lack the dynamism to excel in both. If a product manager is highly skilled at analytical thinking, she is likely to have good technical knowledge and be strong in product and data organization. Often these types of product managers are not at all proactive about speaking to customers or colleagues. If a product manager has a highly people-focused skill-set, she is likely to love spending time with customers and less likely to excel in grasping the detail of the data and software that will deliver what customers want. This type of product manager is also less likely to push back when colleagues and customers ask for development that is outside of the strategic focus of the product roadmap.

The very best product managers and owners have a balance of analytical and people skills and are good decision-makers capable of persuading others. Similar tradeoffs exist in most product owner roles. Product managers and product owners with dynamic analytical and communication skills should be treated as magical unicorns, and when you find them in your organization, you should compensate them highly and empower them to make decisions.

Let's look at an example to illustrate the point. Jamie is a product manager for Essays Online, a product in Acme's Publishing Division that provides online education services. Customers of Essays Online use the software to submit school reports, and after each essay is submitted, a teacher emails a report of what the student did well and what needs to be improved along with the student's grade. All of this collaboration is done online via a web platform. Essays Online users have been asking for an enhancement to the software to enable teachers and students to track progress natively in the platform. Jamie speaks to student users of Essays Online's platform and determines that they want to be notified when a teacher leaves feedback. From there, they want to message the teacher when they have made the suggested improvements. They want to be notified when the teacher accepts or rejects the change.

Teachers also want to be able to extract summary data regarding their students, like how many of their students were graded eighty percent or higher, for example. Jamie does his market research and suspects that Essays Online could justify a price increase if this feature is delivered. He presents the business case to his leadership, and this feature is approved to go on the roadmap. A product owner, Ella, is assigned to take the feature into sprint. Jamie explains what he has heard from customers to Ella, who then writes up the requirements and sticks the features into her scrum team's backlog. The scrum team uploads teacher reports, previously sent as email attachments, to the software system as PDFs with basic data associated with them: date, teacher's name, student's name, and score. Three months later, she shows Jamie what has been built. Indeed, student users can see their reports in the platform, and teachers can pull a list of how many students scored over eighty percent. But when Jamie starts to play around with the feature, he finds that it is limited.

He goes back to Ella: "Hey, can we add a metric where teachers can see not only the individual scores, but also how many students have outstanding actions? Could teachers search for all reports that contain a specific phrase?"

Ella: "Technically, yes, but it will take just as long as the previous feature, because the data aren't stored that way. The information you want the user to be able to see in the platform is stored in a PDF in the database. It isn't easy to access."

Jamie: "Seriously? Another three months just to add a few data fields to the dashboard?"

Ella: "Yes. If you wanted lots of data on the dashboard, you should have said so from the outset. I can't read your mind."

Jamie: "You are always going on and on about keeping our requirements *lean*! 'Start with an MVP' you always say. So, I kept my mouth shut."

Jamie is disappointed and can't understand why the software is unable to break up the information into little pieces. Wasn't it obvious that users were always going to want more elements on the dashboard? Ella is frustrated because she has been working hard on this feature for three months, and her product manager is still not satisfied.

Now, let's replay that example if Jamie and Ella work in slightly more dynamic ways: Jamie explains what he has heard from customers to Ella, who in turn sits down with the information architect (IA), user experience lead (UX), and scrum master from her team. They brainstorm the best way to design and deliver a flexible feature that will allow students and teachers to access individual pieces of data that are stored separately in the database.

The IA asks Ella, "What are all of the possible data fields users might want to access in the platform?" Ella responds, "I don't know. Let me have a look at some sample reports, and I'll work up a list." Ella takes her list to Jamie. Jamie thinks it looks good but wants to put it in front of some customers just to be sure. He arranges some meetings with that list and the clickable prototype the UX lead has put together to gather feedback. Based on those meetings, Ella maps out a process flow of how they expect users to interact with the platform. The IA designs a dynamic data set that will make it much easier to adjust what is on the dashboard in future. The scrum master offers suggestions for how the design could be adjusted to make coding it easier.

Three months later, Jamie starts to play around with the new feature, which is in testing. Of course it still isn't perfect, but when he goes back to Ella and asks: "Hey, can we add a metric where teachers can see not only the individual scores, but also how many students have outstanding actions? Could teachers search for all reports that contain a specific phrase?" Ella responds: "Yes, it should be pretty straightforward. I'll need to wait for capacity to open up, but let me write it up, and we'll see when we can drop it in. In the meantime, are we happy to release this version as it is?" Jamie: "Yes. That sounds ok."

The difference between these two scenarios sits primarily in Ella's curiosity and critical thinking. She wants to understand what users are trying to accomplish with the feature – not just what has been described by Jamie. She takes the time to work with IA to ensure the data design is flexible. She shares prototypes with stakeholders to ensure it will work for the users that want the feature. She accepts and is prepared for the fact that there will inevitably be adjustments to be made after the feature goes into testing.

One way to encourage this behavior is to require product managers, product owners, and information architects to agree on the data fields available in the UI before any technical design or coding commences. They need to specify which data fields are required for the initial release and which data fields could possibly be needed in the future. This will prompt early conversations about future expectations of what information is important to end users. It will ensure that the data on which features are built are structured appropriately. Lean-Agile principles do not explicitly address this point because new products don't usually rely on masses of underlying data. Thinking about data up front is more critical for companies with more history.

Product owners can have a huge, positive impact on the design of features by working proactively and closely with information and database architects to design the underlying shape of data that will be used to power the platform. What is all too common is a scenario in which the data design is a by product of technical or solution architecture, rather than a separately considered artifact that is a precondition for solution design. In these cases, solution designers craft a technical solution, usually something to do with APIs moving data from one place to another, without a full view of how different data structures will hinder or enable future development. The more efficient way to land on a scalable technical design is for the data design to be treated as a prerequisite of equal importance to the solution design. The two should work hand in hand, and the quality of expertise required to craft each should be given equal consideration.

# Key Takeaways

- Chunky corporates want predictable performance.

- Innovation is risky and dilutes margins.

- Product managers and owners leverage people skills to manage collaboration and analytical skills to make evidence-based product decisions.

- Data design should be given as much attention as technical design.

# CHAPTER 3

# Scaling Up

How do companies go from lean startups to chunky corporates? There is a logical transition in which the values of the business shift as the company scales. Often this shift is intangible. It happens relatively organically and is a result of a couple of common, confluent events happening when an organization grows dramatically:

1. **The organization gets bigger.** More products and more teams require more sophisticated communication.

2. **The organization attracts investment.** Investors put pressure on the organization to pursue growth while minimizing risk. Predictability of performance displaces radical innovation.

## Getting Bigger

Lewis Hamilton, a famous Formula One racing car driver, said in 2019, "If I'm one kilogram overweight, I can lose up to two seconds in the race distance." Every kilogram added to either him or the car slows the car down. A similar phenomenon can be observed when a team of Agile developers mature. As a company transitions from lean to chunky, it adds scrum teams. A lean startup will have one development team. Mid-sized chunky corporates typically have between five and ten development teams. Very large organizations can have over one hundred development

© Katie Tamblin 2024
K. Tamblin, *The Lean-Agile Dilemma*, https://doi.org/10.1007/979-8-8688-0321-5_3

teams operating at any one time. The extra weight impacts performance, slowing down decision-making and fomenting inefficiency. But how does this happen?

As a lean startup matures, there is a badge of honor associated with getting bigger. It is a common response for a startup to find confidence in heft. If a startup can afford to add more people, more teams, more developers, it must mean they are on the right path, right? At a minimum, the startup can invest more in software development. It follows logically that the company must be doing well. In the early days, that is usually what it means. However, just because you can afford to add resources, it doesn't necessarily mean those resources will add value at the same rate.

The best analogy I can think of in which a person is excited to gain weight is pregnancy. When I was pregnant, I excitedly jumped on the scales daily – especially in the early days – knowing that putting on weight meant baby was growing healthily. My partner and I took weekly pictures, belly to belly, to see the point at which mine got bigger than his. This started out as funny, but by the end, when my belly was the size of a small planet, it started to feel overwhelming and a bit scary.

Developing and growing a product has some, if perhaps anatomically tenuous, parallels to growing a child. Ladies don't typically get pregnant until their bodies are ready to grow a child; if they are too lean, or too young, it won't happen. Similarly, in the early days of a startup, there is rarely enough cash to invest in additional development resources, or sales teams, or customer support, or anything else. Most employees at a startup wear many hats.

For example, Acme was founded by two colleagues, Rohit and Norman. As there were only two of them, they split all the work between them. Each one had about twelve different jobs. Norman was primarily responsible for delivery of the products, technology, and service solutions. Rohit was primarily responsible for contracts, pricing, and new business generation. There wasn't enough revenue coming in to justify hiring any additional team members in the early days. As revenue grew, though, capacity to grow the team increased.

When pregnant, if things are going well, investment of extra resources is needed for the little one to grow. For me, personally, this looked like double helpings of chocolate brownies and ice cream being a perfectly reasonable daily addition to my diet. For Norm and Ro, double daily brownies took the form of hiring people in various parts of the organization. This felt great to Norm and Ro. Like an expecting mother, they were optimistic and excited to see growth materializing; it represented success and bred confidence in the future of the business.

There is a greater chance that a business will leave a legacy if it is strong enough to grow. With these exciting changes to the form and structure of the organization come some growing pains. Just like a pregnant body, the frame of a startup hasn't had to support extra bodies before, and it can often creak under the strain. As an expecting mum will start to complain of aching hips and stretch marks, Norm and Ro found themselves moaning that things didn't happen as fast as they did in Acme's early days when it was just the two of them. Ro complains he spends all of his time managing the newly hired employees. Norm drifts further and further away from his passion for coding with each new layer of management beneath him.

Norm and Ro experienced this mightily as Acme grew. They hired employees to manage technology and infrastructure for the business. After a few months, Norm and Ro felt frustrated. These new hires were not as efficient at delivery nor as strategically minded as Norm. They thought adding employees would free up their time to focus more on scaling the business, but they underestimated how much time they would spend training and managing new team members. To Norm and Ro, managing felt like watching other people do their jobs less well than they did. For many startup founders, this is painfully true. The time spent hiring and firing until you find the right team creates drag on the organization. A kilo here, a few pounds there, and before you know it, you are losing seconds on your lap time. As this phenomenon continues, organizations traverse the arc of maturation from lean to chunky.

The sheer volume of relationships between colleagues across an organization makes a chunky corporate more difficult to manage. A key difference between a chunky corporate and a lean startup is in the number of employees, with lean startups having few, and chunky corporates having many. Yuval Noah Harari, in his book, *Sapiens: A Brief History of Humankind,*[1] summarizes sociological research demonstrating that large groups of people require a shared set of values, priorities, and identity to collaborate effectively. Small groups can work using intimate relationships and direct communication. Large groups, though, require formal discipline, processes, and oversight to be successful. A typical lean startup will have fewer than ten employees, which works out to a maximum of forty-five relationships to manage between colleagues. For a company with one hundred employees, there are roughly five thousand relationships to manage. Forty-five relationships are relatively straightforward to manage. Managing five thousand relationships requires a completely different toolkit.

In the early days of a lean startup, developers and product leaders work closely with the founders of the business. The right employees, with the right guidance, can learn a great deal by trial and error, moving quickly and developing new features at pace. Growth in a startup brings more customers, and more customers need more customer support. Customers ask for enhancements, which sit alongside features that the development team was planning to build before those customers showed up. This creates decision points where management must say no to customers, drop what was previously planned, or add resources to accomplish both in the same timeframe. In either scenario, the pace of change is impacted.

Norm, Acme's founder and lead product decision-maker, feels conflicted. If he chooses to deliver all of the enhancements requested by Acme's growing customer base, he will sacrifice development on the features he thinks are important: there is a new product line he

---

[1] Harari, Yuval Noah. *Sapiens: A Brief History of Humankind.* Vintage Publishing, 2015.

wants to launch; there is technical debt piling up; Ro has asked him to build workflows that support the new sales team. If Norm chooses to add development resources, he may be able to deliver against more of these demands, but he will still experience drag. Norm assumes if he grows the tech development team proportionately, Acme can spend the same amount of resources on new features while providing appropriate maintenance of existing features. But that isn't what happens.

The pace of delivery slows as the team grows. Norm starts with a team of nine developers. Over time, he finds that five of the nine spend all of their time maintaining existing features and infrastructure, rather than developing new features. He calculates his innovation output has been reduced by roughly fifty-six percent. So, he adds a new team, made up of five developers, that are entirely responsible for maintenance only. The first bit of drag on team performance Norm experiences is during the onboarding of these five new developers. The existing team of nine developers experiences a short-term dip in output while these new team members onboard.

For a period of time after this, additional resources free up time for the "new features" team of nine to focus on building new, like they did before. However, for every new feature built, more work is added to the "maintenance" team's backlog. Eventually, the maintenance team of five is no longer able to maintain all of the features built by their nine colleagues. Over a number of years, you'll find that the amount of time spent on maintenance begins to eclipse the amount of time spent on new features. The older the team, the more time they have had to develop features. The more features they have developed, the larger the burden of maintenance.

# Attracting Investment

There are not many more exciting things than securing your first external investment as a startup. To Norm and Ro, it is validation of the work they invested in setting up Acme and making it successful. They sell the majority of their shares in Acme to a private equity company, who we will refer to as PE. Different types of investors have different appetites for risk, and I won't pretend that the generalizations I am about to make are true of all investors. But, with that caveat in mind, it is a fair generalization that when investor money flows in, risk appetites start to change. This is certainly true of PE's acquisition of Acme.

With external investment comes oversight. PE installs a Board, with Don as its Chairman, and two PE partners as Board members who sit alongside Don in guiding Acme's leadership team. The creation of a Board brings experience and credibility to Acme's growing organization. It alters the culture. How oversight will alter the fabric of an organization is something very few entrepreneurs think about in the beginning when a Board is appointed. Culture change is something that often goes unnoticed while it is happening. It is much easier to see in retrospect. Norm and Ro reflect on Acme's transformation twelve months after having attracted PE investment.

Via regular reporting to the Board, Norm and Ro put processes into place to ensure their growth translates into predictable performance. Revenue growth continues, and as the business grows, it becomes harder and harder to maintain the same percentage growth rates. Ten percent annual revenue growth on a $2 million a year base is $200,000. Ten percent annual revenue growth on $10 million is $1 million. Norm and Ro quickly realize that each year the absolute volume of sales against which they are targeted is growing in leaps and bounds. A bigger number requires a bigger sales team. A bigger sales team builds a bigger customer base. The bigger customer base demands more software features, creating more feature decision points. The flywheel of growth is taking on a life of its own.

Knaster and Leffingwell refer to this in *SAFe Distilled: Achieving Business Agility with the Scaled Agile Framework*: "Taking on these responsibilities requires gaining expertise, hiring specialists, forming departments for efficiency, and developing policies and procedures to ensure legal compliance and driving repeatable, cost-efficient operations. As a result, businesses start to organize by function. Silos begin to form."[2]

Inevitably, there comes a point in which a startup starts to hear the word cost from its Board. Perhaps revenue growth has plateaued. Perhaps the focus on innovation has let costs grow faster than revenue. Controlling cost is not a bad thing, not at all. It is an important part of achieving predictable performance and a critical metric for investors. But when cost control is on the table, innovation goes out the window. Innovation requires inherent risk-taking, and most innovation is margin diluting in the short-term.

If the business can achieve predictable growth with the existing product set, there is simply little-to-no incentive for a Board to empower a business to invest in innovation. When the distance between Acme's revenue curve and its cost curve starts to shrink, Norm and Ro find themselves having a difficult conversation with Acme's Board. The Board want to cut costs. The spend on new product features is too large. PE wants to move ninety percent of development resources on to platform maintenance and eliminate the rest.

Not long after, Norm gets bored and takes a job with another startup. Ro hangs on for another six months, then, like Norm, departs the world of predictable performance for something with more freedom. Norm and Ro realize in retrospect it was at the point the cost conversation was introduced that Acme's corporate culture shifted away from innovation and toward focus.

Was it truly inevitable that the distance between Acme's cost curve and revenue curve would shrink? Well, maybe it is not inevitable, but the longer the investment time horizon, the more likely it becomes. Startup organizations do not fear extra weight. They are not concerned as they scale up because they assume having the resources to scale up means they

---

[2] Knaster, Richard, and Leffingwell, Dean. *SAFe Distilled: Achieving Business Agility with the Scaled Agile Framework.* 5.0. Addison-Wesley, 2020.

are performing well. They assume they will benefit from economies of scale. They assume revenue will continue to outpace growth in cost base. These assumptions are where most companies go wrong.

# Economies of Scale

Economies of scale are *proportionate savings in costs gained by an increased level of production.* A short definition would state that a system is achieving economies of scale when the average cost of production falls as production rises. For every widget produced, the average cost of producing a widget falls. When an organization continues to add resources after reaching the optimal point of production, the organization will experience diseconomies of scale. Diseconomies of scale refer to the scenario in which the average cost of production is rising for each equivalent unit of output.

Economies of scale are most traditionally understood, recognized, and explained by the presence of specialization and machinery. The more complex our tools have become – and particularly as they evolved into what we call machines – the greater the ratio of output to input is.

Let's take the printing press as an example. For hundreds of years, humans operated in cultures with written traditions scribbled by individual hand. What started as cave drawings or perhaps etchings on wood or stone evolved into written letters on paper. This became significantly more efficient with the introduction of the quill, but, still, it required a person to write each letter for each publication. On average, a person could write three to four pages a day with a quill.

With the invention of the printing press, however, there came a process: up-front investment of time to set the letters in the appropriate pattern meant that the first page took longer than a traditional handwritten page. However, thousands of pages could be printed in quick succession once that upfront investment was complete. The Guttenberg printing press could print up to 3,600 pages per day. This meant that with an initial infusion of capital – money to purchase a printing press and time to set the letters into the appropriate patterns – a much greater yield of output (in this case, pages printed) could be achieved. Over time, the scale of page output per day greatly outweighed the upfront investment. This meant the cost per page was dramatically reduced – resulting in economy of scale. If a printer were to only print one page, a printing press would be substantially less efficient than writing by hand. The benefit is only realized when operating at scale.

This concept holds with the vast majority of machines, including computing machines and computers. Businessmen and women the world over have made the assumption that this concept also holds in the production of software. Here, though, I'd like to question the premise. Do economies of scale naturally hold when applied to an effort of human coordination such as that required to build a complex web platform?[3] It appears to be a fundamental assumption of mature organizations' management that if you need more software functionality, adding more developers to a software project will deliver more features in a shorter space of time. This would make each unit of code less costly than the last, under the principle of economies of scale. However, identifying a common unit of code *output* is much more complex than counting how many widgets were manufactured in a day.

Code has its own innate efficiencies rendering the comparison fruitless. A software feature could have thousands of lines of code but not provide any additional value to customers. We cannot measure the effective output of software by the number of lines of code written, nor the number of features delivered. It is more complicated than that. The attachment of individual software features to business outcomes is the

---

[3] For the purposes of this argument, we will ignore shared functions, such as Human Resources (HR), Marketing, and Finance, and focus specifically on how well the concept of economies of scale holds within the process of software development. We are concerned, here, with whether the concept of economies of scale holds in the context of the creation of software, not whether it holds in the context of software use.

most effective way to determine if software is efficient. However, most chunky corporates do not take the time to do this. In fairness to them, this is really time-consuming and hard to do. Most teams wouldn't know where to start, which, in and of itself, is one of our biggest challenges. If you don't know how to measure success, how do you know you are building good software applications? As it is complex and messy to assign business outcomes to individual software features, the effectiveness of software is usually measured holistically by how well an entire web platform supports revenue and profit growth for the company.

Economies of scale-based thinking follows the concept of a factory or assembly line: hundreds of colleagues work alongside each other effectively. Want more cars? Add more assembly lines. In the factory scenario, workers are performing discrete tasks repeatedly. This allows for simplistic scaling up of resources. When building something complex like a car, the design is sophisticated, and it comes first. A team of engineers create a steadfast design for the car that will be built. That design has clear objectives for each discrete part of the car. Once agreed and rigorously tested, very few material changes are made to the design. The individuals on the assembly line do not have the skills required to change the design of the item being produced nor do they have the freedom to do so. They work to an existing design: assembling predefined parts into a final product. They repeat an action to provide as many copies of the product as possible. Variation in the product is minimized.

Software development is fundamentally a different enterprise. Software developers are the engineers. To apply the principle of a factory, imagine if every assembly line worker was an engineer. Imagine rather than a steadfast design and a series of pre-fabricated parts, the assembly line worker was given a rough description of what a car is, then told to build a specific component, like a steering column. That engineer might build the fanciest, most impressive steering column in the world, but there would be very little likelihood that the steering column would have any, impact on the operation of the wheels.

Large scale software development can often feel like you let the engineers loose on an assembly line. There are hundreds of decision points that cannot be predicted in the design phase but present themselves during the development process. At each decision point, the engineer, or software developer, writing the code, must either make a decision quickly or speak to colleagues to align around the appropriate decision. Nine times out of ten, the engineer will make a decision. You can't fault the engineer for that. She likely has a target of completed user stories to be delivered, and asking permission takes longer. Our efficiency-seeking incentives make it harder for the developer to speak to colleagues when decision points arise. Collaboration would slow down the writing of code. The developer discounts the future inefficiency of making a poor decision in favor of delivering code. The bigger the team, the more opportunities for misalignment. These design decisions made in-build can take the feature further away from its intended purpose.

Code writing is not a discrete, repetitive task, like assembling a car. Writing code is a task of engineering, which opposed to assembly, operates on different principles, leaving large software projects more open to diseconomies of scale. Once a software project has passed beyond the point of optimal capacity, each additional developer will produce fewer equivalent code units than the previous. The reason I say "equivalent code" is that not all code is considered equal. Each incremental developer may write the same number of lines of code, but if that code doesn't work effectively, it is not delivering economies of scale.

Thousands of lines of code can be wasted when they are not joined up to the rest of the platform, do not deliver on the business outcome attached to the feature, or when they are riddled with design gaps. The more people you add, the more difficult it becomes to align resources. The bigger the project, the more hand-offs between people. Hand-offs require explicit and precise communication. You cannot scale that sort of process in the same way you invest in a printing press. The concept doesn't transfer to coding because even with detailed architectural designs, there are a hundred different ways you could code the same function.

Let's revisit the example of building a car. The first car was built before the assembly line was put in place. Then, the car was taken apart, and the various build elements were itemized and separated into discrete tasks that could be repeated by workers on the assembly line. The difference in writing code is that you hope to only build it once. When you have multiple teams working on coding a single platform, it is the equivalent of putting one team on building a chassis, another on the steering mechanism, another on the gearbox, another on the wheels and then hoping that when they all finish, they can fit the pieces together to form the first car. The only way the car assembly works is with a detailed design that has been repeatedly honed through a process of assembling the first few "test" cars. The software equivalent of a "test" car is a proof of concept, but, by their nature, proofs of concept are not comprehensive enough to identify all of the decisions individual engineers will make throughout the build.

If scaling up your platform build means adding more teams, you run the risk of offsetting most of your resource gains by introducing inefficiencies of communication between teams. Humans communicate best in small teams. Scrums reflect this. I have actually observed software builds go faster when teams are removed. Remaining teams will spend less time fitting various elements together, less time filling in gaps between the applications, and more time just getting on with building the core features required.

Software companies reach *optimal capacity* of engineers working on a single platform pretty early in the scaling up process. However, most do not realize this. As a result, the maturity curve of a software company looks like that in Figure 3-1.

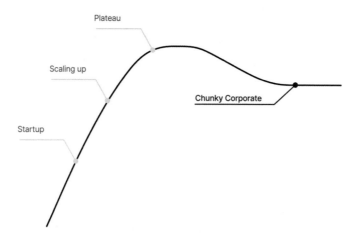

**Figure 3-1.** *The software business maturity curve*

The company starts out lean and agile, as a result of constrained resources. It survives those fraught early days, demonstrating growth and attracting investment. It scales up, adding teams of developers (and sales, and customer support, and marketing, and product, and so on). It hits a performance plateau in which costs continue rising while revenue stagnates. A self-aware chunky corporate pivots at the point of reaching a performance plateau, recognizing that optimal capacity of product development has been reached. At that point, the company needs to do one of two things: reset revenue expectations for flatter growth, or focus on unlocking efficiency via smart deployment of product and technology. The former is incompatible with the expectations of investor/owners. Therefore, efficient, optimized product and technology resources must become the competitive edge at a company facing a performance plateau.

There is an inflection point in every business at which innovation-based product development must give way to focused execution to continue delivering growth. When organizations miss this inflection point and continue to develop using Lean-Agile principles based on trial-and-error heavy innovation, growth stagnates. In 2023, many technology giants hit this phase of the software maturity curve. Telltale signs of shareholder pressure, layoffs, and a generally disgruntled workforce demonstrate that even the greats: Google, Meta, Microsoft, Apple,  the company formerly known as Twitter, Tesla, and Amazon, can fall victim to diminishing returns when they hit middle age.[4] Different companies reach this plateau on different timelines. Some, like Apple and Microsoft, have been up and down this curve multiple times.

Between being a lean startup and scaling up, revenues rise faster than costs, making the organization an attractive investment. Between scaling up and hitting a performance plateau, however, the organization passes optimal capacity and starts to falter. Diminishing returns set in. The more colleagues the organization adds, the lower the incremental output it achieves with each one. If the organization fails to realize it has reached and is now moving beyond optimal capacity, its performance will falter. Costs continue rising as revenue flattens. Profits begin to contract, leading to shareholder pressure, layoffs, and a disgruntled workforce.

This can be mitigated, to some degree, by two things: (1) paying close attention to optimal capacity and (2) investing heavily in software design as you scale the engineering team. It is hard to see optimal capacity until you have passed it. The challenges Acme is experiencing – poor communication, vague objectives for software features, misalignment across functional silos – are indicative of a company operating beyond optimal engineering capacity. Dynamic and informed key performance indicators (KPIs) or objectives and key results (OKRs) can identify the point at which an organization has reached optimal capacity.

Unrealistically long backlogs, tension between software and product resources, and missed deadlines indicate the team is operating at or just beyond optimal capacity. Adding engineers to a team already struggling

---

[4] Hynes, Dan. "Here's What Feels Different about Big Tech Redundancies in the New Era of 'Loud Firing,'" April 11, 2023. https://atomico.com/insights/dan-hynes-tech-redundancies.

to deliver on business outcomes is unlikely to help. Instead of investing in additional engineers, Acme should invest more resources in design. Acme needs to ensure product leaders focus on the right products to enable predictable growth and that the design of those products enables them to be delivered in a measured and efficient way.

When operating near or beyond optimal capacity, software design requires more attention than writing code. At a company that has already scaled up, specialist roles deliver technical and architectural design. The challenge many chunky corporates have is that these roles are spread thinly across multiple scrum teams and are not involved in end-to-end development. They are merely inserted between specification of requirements and software coding and rarely can see the big picture of how an ecosystem of applications hangs together. This makes it incredibly difficult for these resources to create designs of a high enough quality and to a deep enough level of detail that will deliver on the aspirations of the business.

A technical design team needs to articulate architecture as detailed as a car design for an assembly line, but they are not given the resources, time, nor information to do that effectively. As a result, software development teams spend an inordinate amount of time filling gaps and reworking edges of software pieces. This is commonly overlooked in the context of adding teams to a software build.

If you want to scale your software team, you must invest in appropriate resources to produce thorough, discrete, and detailed designs that scrums respect. By eliminating, or at least reducing, the in-build design decisions that have to be made by engineers, you stand the best chance of limiting the inherent inefficiencies associated with scaling up a software engineering function.

# Key Takeaways

- When a company transitions from lean to chunky, volumes of human relationships across the business increase exponentially.

- Software development teams experience diseconomies of scale when they grow beyond optimal capacity.

- Larger software teams require disproportionate investment in design over engineering to maximize efficiency.

# CHAPTER 4

# Chief Poo-Poo Officer and Saying No

---

**Note**  *A Chief Product Officer (CPO) is a corporate title referring to an executive who leads the product organization. A CPO is responsible for the strategic product direction. Usually, it includes product vision, product innovation, product design, product development, project management, and product marketing.*

—Product Plan[1]

---

Colleagues of mine once joked that my title, CPO, really stood for Chief Poo-Poo Officer, rather than Chief Product Officer. My role primarily involved saying no: No, we aren't going to deliver that. No, that's not on the roadmap. No, that's not worth our time. No, that's a terrible idea. No, that business case isn't strong enough. No, that's not our priority.

It's a title I have come to embrace. Many chunky corporates need a Chief Poo-Poo Officer. A multitude of product sins originate with saying yes to every request. A Chief Poo-Poo Officer relies on focus to drive growth. Lack of focus in the product stack results in fragmentation.

---

[1] "Product Plan," n.d. www.productplan.com/glossary/chief-product-officer/.

© Katie Tamblin 2024
K. Tamblin, *The Lean-Agile Dilemma*, https://doi.org/10.1007/979-8-8688-0321-5_4

Focus, on the other hand, can return shrinking sales to growth. It can drive down the cost base and drive up profitability. It is the role of product to determine where technology resources should focus. Product-led strategy is critical to continued success of mature businesses.

Product, as a business function, is responsible for balancing the needs and wants of both internal and external customers with the feasibility of delivery and the performance goals of the company. It is the fundamental role of product to gather information from customers, sales, marketing, operations, finance, and technology. From that input, the product team determines the appropriate balance of priorities that will deliver growth to the business, serve the needs of customers, and not overwhelm the technology team with an unrealistic set of requirements. It sounds simple, right? In reality, it means saying no to the majority of requests received.

Lev, the VP of Product in Acme's Survey division, joined the company six months ago. As soon as he joined, he started to hear complaints that the software development team dedicated to Survey Division were underperforming. As he investigates these, he finds that there is a long backlog of software enhancement requests submitted by colleagues and customers of Survey Division. Customers and colleagues alike complain that software enhancement requests go into a black hole never to be heard from again.

Lev asks the team about the process used to manage incoming requests for changes to the software platform. He finds that every request must be submitted via an online form. Requests submitted online are reviewed weekly by a multi-functional team, called the Customer Advisory Board (CAB). If there is enough information and good reason to pursue the request, the technology team estimates the effort (in units of both time and cost) required to deliver it. Lev asks one of the members of CAB to provide him with insights regarding the number of requests coming in, how quickly they are actioned, and the average time between submission, approval, and delivery. What he finds is staggering.

Survey Division has just over 600 employees, and the CAB received over 450 requests in the previous twelve months. Some of the requests for product enhancements are estimated to take months to build. The Survey Division technology team cannot possibly deliver successfully on 1.25 requests a day. The list of un-actioned requests is in the hundreds. Of the requests that were approved, the time between submission and execution varies widely. Changes that require code releases, on average, take more than twelve months to go from request to delivery. Some requests have been on the waiting list for more than three years!

Lev presents his findings to LaTonya, Survey Division's CEO. She looks bamboozled. "How did we end up here?" She asks. "How on earth could we have reasonable requests for software changes or new features coming in at more than one a day?"

Lev: "I know I'm still pretty new here, but from what I can see, we are blurring the lines between fixed products and custom software. Customer success and sales colleagues view the software products as malleable – something that can be customized to reflect the individual needs of each customer. However, we are not charging commensurate fees to reflect that. Our pricing strategy is built on fixed products: something you build once and sell over and over again. That combination is killing our margins. We do not have the resources to deliver the customization expected. Customers are getting grumpy."

LaTonya: "That explains recent cancellations. Customer expectations are out of line with what the team can deliver."

Lev: "We have to move to a single, consistent product stack. The legacy of customizing the platform has left us with a maintenance overhead that the technology team cannot support. We need repeatable products that can be sold at scale to get business performance back on track."

LaTonya: "How do we get from here to there?"

Lev: "We have to start saying no. This is going to be a painful change for colleagues who are not well-trained in managing customer requests effectively. Products need to be defined, and I'm going to need your help in enforcing strict controls on any change or enhancement requests. We have to work down this backlog of un-actioned requests. We have to communicate with our customers to tell them a lot of this simply isn't going to be delivered. We have to make it clear why and then manage their expectations."

LaTonya: "Ugh. This sounds painful."

Lev: "Yep – it probably will be. I need your support, LaTonya. You have to take the lead on changing the culture. I'll get to work with the technology team on changing the strategy to be product-led. When we get the technology and product teams focused on building scalable, repeatable products, that will drive margin expansion. However, we have to also align the sales and customer management functions to setting expectations accordingly. There is no use fixing our cost base if we cannot expand revenue alongside it."

Lev and LaTonya are facing a change journey. They must retrain their teams to think about products as fixed things that customers can purchase as they are, with discretely defined configurable pieces. LaTonya must lead a journey of understanding across her team and enable her colleagues to then take customers on the same journey.

Currently, Survey Division's company culture enables its customers to treat software like they would order a birthday cake from a boutique bakery: "Yes, can I get three layers, please? One chocolate and two vanilla. I'd like white frosting, and can you please write: 'Happy Birthday, Violet' on the top? Oh, and I'd like a unicorn horn made out of meringue, too please – with glitter sparkles of edible sugar."

LaTonya and Lev must teach Survey Division's colleagues and customers to think about our products like they were picking out a cake at a grocery store, not ordering from a fancy bakery. At the grocery store, you can have the chocolate one or the vanilla one. Each one is already baked and boxed up with a price tag and description on the box. You don't get much choice, but it is cheaper and simpler (plus the baker records higher profits). Lev and LaTonya need to explain this concept of a product-led business and how the products will be scalable and repeatable rather than highly customized. However, it is not so easy to translate that conversation into changes in behavior.

It is one thing to define a new vision for an organization. But teaching individuals how to apply that vision to their daily activities is hard work at a chunky corporate, particularly when the culture is based on years of *how it has always been done*. Moving from a company culture used to saying, "Yes, we can customize that for you" to a culture that says, "No, the product doesn't do that" is difficult. Survey Division colleagues need to get comfortable saying no. No is hard in the short term. People don't like being told no, and people don't like saying no, but no is important. No is honest. No is better in the long run. People may not like hearing no at the outset. However, what they like even less is being told yes and then being disappointed because the yes was never delivered. Let's walk through two scenarios to illustrate the point.

Diego is an account manager in Acme's Survey Division. One of his big accounts is Globus Corp. He has a good relationship with Danielle, his key point of contact at Globus. Danielle comes to him to say the rollout of the product is going well, but she has had feedback from the users that they'd like to be able to send messages to each other within the platform. Diego responds to her request: "That sounds like a really interesting idea. No, it can't do that today, but I'll talk to the team to see when we could add that feature to the roadmap." Diego submits a request to add this feature to the platform via the usual process, and this goes to the CAB for review. The technology team estimates that the feature would take six sprints, or twelve weeks, for one team to build. The roadmap is full; no one knows when the team would get around to building it.

The CAB asks Diego if the customer is willing to fund the development, but he doesn't know. The product team reaches out to other customers to see if anyone else is interested in messaging. The response is "meh." No one thinks it is a bad idea, but no one can really justify putting other features on hold in order to make room in the roadmap for this request.

After all, this is just one customer, and the platform supports hundreds of customers like Globus. So, the request goes to the end of the list. Maybe the team will build it someday when the list is shorter.

Months go by. Danielle asks Diego what is happening with messaging. Diego says he doesn't know, but he'll check. Now Diego is feeling the pressure. He kinda suggested in the initial conversation that messaging would get built at some point. Now he is not so sure. He worries he will upset Danielle if he tells her that. He doesn't want to upset his customer and risk injuring their relationship. More months go by. Danielle feels like the product is under-delivering. She has in her mind that messaging was promised to her as a future feature, and she has heard nothing about it. Danielle is growing disgruntled.

Let's look at another way Diego could have handled Danielle's feedback. Diego responds to Danielle: "That's a really interesting point. The product doesn't support messaging. I can speak to the product team to see if that is on the roadmap already, or if it would require additional investment. I can come back to you with a cost estimate and a timeline if it is a feature that would add value to your use of the platform." Danielle responds, "Thanks, Diego, that would be great. I'm not sure it is something we'd be willing to pay for, or have budget for, but I appreciate your asking."

A couple of weeks later, Diego comes back to Danielle: "Hi, Danielle – so sorry to be the bearer of bad news, but messaging isn't currently on the roadmap, and it sounds like a pretty big piece of work to deliver it. I am happy to walk you through the details of the feature enhancements we are working on instead. I would also like to set up some time for us to discuss it in more detail with our product team, so they can understand the benefits of that feature to you. They can provide a quotation for what it would cost to build it and when it would be possible to schedule it for delivery." Danielle responds, "Thanks, Diego – no worries – it isn't a feature that we would be willing to fund. Instead, we've set up a dedicated Teams channel so we can share messages on the topic, which is working well."

Which scenario ends with Diego and Danielle's relationship remaining positive and getting stronger? The answer is the second one. It may have felt counterintuitive that saying no to Danielle would result in building a stronger relationship, but the reality is that saying yes when you don't have control over whether or not the team can deliver what you've just promised is a much more dangerous play.

Asking a customer to put a value on the request: "What budget would you set aside to fund this custom development?" encourages the customer to think about how important the request is. Customers ask for stuff all the time. Not all customer requests are equal. The important factor is how much the related development is worth to the customer and how many other customers would benefit from it. A responsible product team will not make promises about future delivery of features whose value to the wider customer base is unproven. Without knowing what the feature is worth to Danielle, the team will struggle to prioritize effectively.

# Here's How to Handle Feature Requests

1. Thank the customer for providing feedback.

2. Ask the customer about the business problem she/he wants to solve with the new feature.

3. Ask the customer if she/he would be willing to fund development of the feature or pay an additional fee to gain access to the feature if it was developed.

4. Explain to the customer that you cannot be sure if the feature is feasible or aligns to the priorities of the product road map but that you will investigate these things and provide a response.

5.  Keep the customer informed. Provide an update, even if the update is "We still don't have a decision," every two to three weeks. If you read point 5 and think, "I couldn't possibly update all of my customers who have asked for enhancements every few weeks," your roadmap lacks focus. Tell your customers awaiting a response "No, that feature enhancement will not be delivered" and clear your slate.

Prioritization of features for development is a critical function that the product team provides for the business. Accurately predicting which features will be used heavily by existing customers and which features will drive customer acquisition can be tricky, to say the least. Lean startups rely on the build-measure-learn loop, but chunky corporates have to prioritize what to build first. Lean startups don't have hundreds of change requests to sift through when deciding what to build. They have a blank sheet and hypotheses regarding existing market opportunities.

Chunky corporates, on the other hand, have customers and colleagues asking for new features every day. By sheer volume alone, it is obvious that product leaders at chunky corporates should be saying no most of the time. The role of a strong product function is to accurately predict which features will enable the business to acquire more customers than it loses. Inevitably that means that niche features that are nice to have rather than must-have for a small set of customers will be ignored. Customers are quite capable of understanding that when it is communicated appropriately. They may not like it, but they are unlikely to be upset if expectations were set accordingly at the outset.

The reason large, mature software businesses establish discrete product functions is entirely to make these difficult decisions. It is the role of product to drive customer focus and deliver solutions that solve customers' problems. Customer-facing colleagues must align to this and trust the product team to deliver on customer needs. Strong communication underpins all of this. It is at the heart of setting appropriate expectations with customers and building a deep understanding of what existing and prospective customers want.

# Staying Focused

Where do product requirements come from? Are they delivered by stork? Not usually. Product requirements come from everywhere and anywhere. Everyone who uses a platform thinks they know best how the platform should be improved. The practical consequence of this is that product requests come flying in from all angles. If you don't have a Chief Poo-Poo Officer to keep the list under control, your chunky corporate is at risk of drowning in product requirements.

The scope of requested enhancements is always greater than the capacity available to deliver them at a chunky corporate. Investor owners logically limit the amount of resources spent on software development at an organization with a mature product stack. It is in the interest of investors to control spending to maximize the value of the business. Spending on software development will be reserved for maintenance of the existing products and the inevitable replatforming project. In particular, investors preparing a business for sale will aim to get technology spending down to between two percent and five percent of total revenue. This leaves very little space in the product roadmap for delivery of product enhancements. But did anybody remember to tell that to the sales team?

Customer-facing colleagues are a common source of product improvement ideas. Well, of course they are: they talk to customers most often and are the most common mouthpiece for customer voice. That is perfectly natural and something product leaders should encourage. However, they should encourage it in a way that makes clear all suggestions from customers and customer-facing colleagues will be considered but not necessarily built. It is imperative that chunky corporates empower product managers to be mini-Poo-Poo Officers. If they do not, customer-facing colleagues will quickly stuff a software backlog beyond a point of reasonable delivery.

Products with the right balance of market demand, revenue potential, feasibility, and cost should get the highest priority on the product roadmap. These are not necessarily the same products colleagues are shouting about. Many of the organizations I've supported have experienced some shape, form, or fashion of a product roadmap lacking in focus. In these cases, the roadmap has been hijacked by poor requirements control. When the roadmap reflects a disparate set of unvalidated requirements, product fragmentation is just around the corner.

The role of product is to investigate every anecdote to determine the Pareto optimal solution, which may be to do nothing. What solutions or features meet the outcome the customer is trying to achieve? Which features drive revenue growth? Which ones meet the needs of the largest amount of customers and prospects for the lowest cost? Unfortunately, remaining focused on identified requirements means product must say no to the sales team.

What happens after product says no to the sales team? Well, next, the sales team needs to say no to the customer. This is not natural or intuitive behavior for most salespeople. They want the path of least resistance to closing deals. The best sales teams are comfortable having this conversation and recognize the value in quickly disqualifying a deal if the customer's requirements do not match Acme's product capabilities. Strong salespeople explain how a customer can achieve business objectives with the existing products, not to get pulled into a conversation about what the product might offer in the future.

I remember a particularly strategic customer, who from our first conversation was always providing suggestions for how to improve the platform. Throughout the sales process, we had deeply valuable conversations about how his team wanted to use the software and how it could be improved. When this customer was onboarded to the platform, he identified a list of over twenty improvement items that he wanted us to address. We wrote down each one, and in our bi-weekly meetings gave updates on each item.

There were some that we did address; they were good suggestions that offered a benefit to all customers on the platform. There were others that we said we would do when time allowed, but we were clear they were not high-enough priority to cause us to alter our product roadmap. And, there were some that we said we wouldn't do. After six months of using the software, the customer said to me, "The rest of the items on this list, you can just ignore. Honestly, most of my feedback was simply coming from a place of ignorance. I didn't know how to use the platform yet; now that I've been using it for six months, most of these changes I see are unnecessary." That, to me, is one of the best endorsements of the role of product I've heard. A good product manager can determine which feedback is valuable and which feedback is going to be obsolete in time. However, even the best product managers struggle with this at times. When teams are under pressure, the quality of decisions related to what the team can feasibly deliver is often the first thing sacrificed.

# Key Takeaways

- When a company scales up, software enhancement requests eventually exceed capacity to deliver them.

- Product managers must be empowered to say no to most requests.

- Customer-facing resources must be trained and managed to set appropriate customer expectations.

# CHAPTER 5

# Deciding What to Build and How

It's a bright and sunny Monday morning, and Cheryl, VP of Product, has assembled her team in the office. Recently, she has been hearing from Caroline, the Head of Delivery for Analytics Division, that the Analytics backlog is a mess. She could hear in Caroline's voice that the scrum teams working on Analytics Division software are feeling overwhelmed. Cheryl has put a half-day workshop in the diary for the team to talk through upcoming priorities.

Included on the invite list are Cheryl's product managers and product owners and Caroline, who serves as the link between the Analytics Division and the software engineers that keep its applications running smoothly. At the start of the meeting, Caroline plugs in her laptop, and a table pops up on the large screen at the front of the room. Most of the team are familiar with this matrix. It is how they manage the various scrum teams' backlogs. Each planned feature has a row. Sprint numbers and dates are populated across the top, and in the cells, resources are assigned to each feature (Figure 5-1).

© Katie Tamblin 2024
K. Tamblin, *The Lean-Agile Dilemma*, https://doi.org/10.1007/979-8-8688-0321-5_5

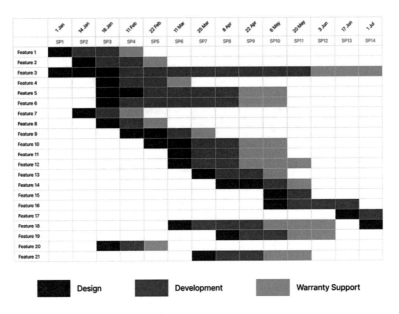

*Figure 5-1.* *Sample sprint plan*

Cheryl has assembled the key players to discuss the current sprint plan and evaluate Caroline's concern. The reporting line for product professionals flows upward into the Analytics Division management team. Cheryl and her product team are, from a reporting line perspective, aligned to the Analytics Division's management team. The reporting line for technology professionals flows upward into Acme's Chief Technology Officer, who serves all divisions. Caroline and her team of software engineers are, from a reporting line perspective, aligned to the Technology function of the business. Information flows up and down these silos via line management.

In the current sprint, sprint 4, technical architect, Sara, is meant to be working with information architect, Ulrich, on the back-end design of the new Productiva profile feature, Feature 9. (This is denoted by the dark blue box in column SP4, row Feature 9.) It is expected to be passed to scrum team Mars in sprint 6. This gives the scrum master, Reijo, two weeks, during sprint 5, to review the feature before his team starts to code it. The profile design is expected to be pretty simple. Sara and Ulrich don't think many questions will arise during the review period.

Also in sprint 4, Team Apollo, with scrum master Ylermi, are working on a new feature (Feature 4) to let users upgrade their subscriptions online. Ulrich and Sara are struggling to complete the design for the profile feature because questions keep coming up about how the subscription upgrade feature should work. Sara and Ulrich know that it is important that the design for the profile gets done in time for Reijo to review before it goes into sprint. But the upgrade feature is being coded right now. So, they prioritize fire-fighting the key questions around the upgrade feature over completing the design of the dashboard feature.

Meanwhile, Kamila, scrum master of team Minerva, has been put on bug fixing (Feature 20), because the requirements for her planned feature, Feature 6, a new analytics dashboard, aren't done yet. Those are sitting with Carmen, product owner. Carmen is waiting on a final product design from Tyson, the user experience (UX) lead.

Confused yet? Well, that's the problem. Scrum masters, architects, design leads, and POs struggle to stay on top of the moving parts and inter-dependencies of this sprint plan. They have become lost. They can no longer distinguish the anchor point of orientation guiding their priorities. Spatial disorientation is a term used in aviation to describe the phenomena when a pilot can no longer differentiate between the vertical and horizontal lines. In brutal laypersons terms, it describes when a pilot can't tell which is up, down, left, or right. Ninety percent of aviation mishaps attributed to spatial disorientation are fatal.[1]

---

[1] Woods, Sabrina. "Blurred Lines: Recognizing the Causes of Spatial Disorientation," n.d. https://iflyamerica.org/medical_recognizing_causes_of_spatial_disorientation.asp#:~:text=Approximately%20243%20mishaps%20are%20attributed,pilots%20and%20passengers%20a%20year.

When a pilot cannot navigate based on a visual point of orientation, she is likely to crash into the ground. Metaphorically, this phenomenon feels like it holds when large groups of software and product colleagues lose their point of orientation as well. Teams need a North Star to guide them and around which they can remain aligned. When we organize their communication and collaboration around reporting lines, rather than the North Star, or end goal of a milestone, we make it harder for groups to navigate in unison.

An organization chart depicts reporting lines, but teams collaborate across the organization, not up and down it. Teams take great pains to map software dependencies in user stories, but very few teams map people dependencies. By creating a visual representation of the key players required for features in the sprint plan, we can more clearly identify the dependencies among them. This is called a stakeholder map. In it, common points of strain emerge where multiple dependencies exist. Figure 5-2 demonstrates what those interdependencies look like in a stakeholder mapping.

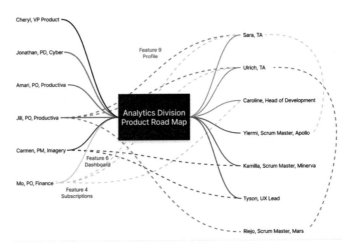

***Figure 5-2.*** *Stakeholder mapping of Analytics Division Sprint Planning*

It looks quite different from an organization chart, doesn't it? The lines show us relationships between stakeholders around a common goal (delivery of the Analytics Division Product Road Map). We ignore their reporting lines because those are irrelevant for the delivery of the Analytics Division sprint plan. Instead, we focus on where collaboration needs to happen to deliver working software which will, in turn, deliver business outcomes. We can see that Sara and Ulrich are critical to the work Mo and Ylermi are preparing for sprint as well as the work Jill and Riejo are preparing for future sprints.

The managers, Cheryl and Caroline, aren't the most critical points in the map. Mapping key stakeholders reveals Sara and Ulrich are critical to success because multiple items depend on them. So, while Cheryl and Caroline are in charge of running the teams, Ulrich and Sara are the bottlenecks. Sara and Ulrich have the most dependencies. The pressure to keep things moving through sprints means that the team do not have adequate time to build and review designs with required stakeholders before pushing features into sprint.

Cheryl stops the conversation: "Ok, I think I'm getting the overall picture. It certainly seems to me that we are off balance. Unexpected questions about features currently in sprint are pulling on resources that are supposed to be working on designs. That leads to incomplete designs of features that are going into sprint. Incomplete designs mean more in-sprint questions. Unless we actively break this cycle, we will end up on a loop yielding poor designs and half-baked features. Anyone disagree?"

There are nods around the room. The team feel under pressure, and they are starting to blame each other.

Kamila: "I can't get this into sprint because Carmen hasn't delivered."

Carmen: "I can't deliver until I get a final design from Tyson, who has spent the last three weeks researching the product design with customers."

Tyson: "It is absolutely imperative that I get market feedback on the optimal design of front-end components."

Carmen: "Christ, Tyson, this isn't Google's DeepMind project. We are rebuilding an existing analytics dashboard page, not sending a rocket to the moon. Back when I started, product designers didn't need a customer to tell us the best way to lay out a page, we hired UI designers because they were the experts!"

Tyson: "In today's episode of dysfunctional workplaces, the part of the grumpy old codger who thinks new ways of working are always wrong will be played by Carmen...."

Carmen: "I am not opposed to change. I just think the evolution in product design research started when a 22-year-old in Silicon Valley figured out that espousing a market research-based doctrine eliminated any need to bring expertise to job role, enabling 22-year-olds to elevate themselves to the same level as grumpy old codgers with 20 years under their belts."

Cheryl: "All right, let's keep it friendly. We are under incredible pressure to deliver a range of milestones. It is up to us to work effectively to manage all of the moving parts."

Despite the tension between Tyson and Carmen, the real issue here is Kamila is not being used to her full capacity, and Caroline feels pressure to get her back in active rotation of feature building. Regardless of whether Tyson's approach to UI/UX design is right or wrong, the fact his design is not signed off in time for Kamila to take it into sprint leads to inefficiency.

In addition, our stakeholder map shows that Ulrich and Sara are managing multiple relationships with product and technology. Because Sara and Ulrich are spread too thinly across multiple areas, the quality of their designs is suffering. Sara and Ulrich cannot effectively work through the volume of designs required to execute the sprint plan. The team can either invest in additional design resources, which won't happen overnight, or reduce the design burden. Reducing the design burden is the only viable short-term solution. The team is on a hamster wheel of inadequate requirements being taken into sprint which is slowing the team down and runs a high risk of introducing tech debt as a result of ill-considered designs. The list of large features requiring design must be reduced immediately so the team can operate effectively.

# Deciding What to Build

Let's get to the root cause of the challenges facing Analytics Division's product team. Tyson, Sara, and Ulrich are a bottleneck. There are too many features planned and not enough design resources to ensure they are executed effectively. The only hope of releasing the bottleneck, in the short term, is to reduce the amount of features requiring design. The team needs to slow down in order to speed up.

Cheryl: "How many different enhancements are we planning to deliver over the next six months?"

Caroline: "Including the small ones? About fifty."

Cheryl: "Fifty new enhancements? Fifty!"

Caroline: "I know. It sounds crazy, but that list of fifty has been whittled down already from the over two hundred requests that have come in over the last year."

Cheryl: "Fifty is not reasonable. If we try to deliver fifty enhancements, we will end up with forty half-baked bits of functionality and a host of customers screaming at us for not delivering the ten we said we could deliver but never got to in the end."

Caroline: "So, what do we do?"

Cheryl: "Get it down to ten. Product managers and product owners, you have to prioritize with more brutality. I would rather deliver ten good enhancements than fifty crappy ones. Plus, I cannot believe we are in a situation in which all fifty enhancements we are trying to deliver are mission-critical in the next six months."

Caroline: "What do we do for sprint 5?"

Cheryl: "Any requirements that are ready for sprint, the teams can take into sprint. Ulrich and Sara need to support Ylermi. Before they kill themselves designing a new Productiva dashboard, let's make sure that is on our top ten. And if there are features for which the business case is not complete, those simply don't make it on to the top ten for this time period. They have to wait until their business cases can be completed appropriately." Cheryl looks at Jill, the product manager.

Jill: "The dashboard is definitely in my top ten. It benefits over 15,000 users and is expected to drive additional revenue of $1 million over the next three years. The sales team is counting on it."

Cheryl: "I am glad you have those numbers at hand. That being said, there will not be a final decision until we've reviewed the list of fifty and determined the top ten as a group. We need that completed before the end of sprint 4. We have three scrum teams. No team should have more than one large feature in their backlog at any given time. We have to stop assuming that a team can move on at the end of their sprint estimate. Any feature given a T-shirt size estimate of L, XL, or XXL is that team's single priority until it is done. I do not want to see teams being assigned to other features until the biggies have been signed off by the business and any critical enhancements are delivered. That means our top ten cannot have more than three L/XL/XXL features in it. We have to get the important features done well before moving on."

Caroline: "If only it was easy to know when a feature is done. And when it is done well."

Cheryl (laughing): "I know. I know. It is difficult when we are under so much pressure. But we are making it harder on ourselves by writing the requirements, then throwing them over a fence for another team to design, who then throws them over a fence for another team to code, who then throws them over the fence for another team to test. We have to tear down the fences and start working more collaboratively. The definition of done must meet the business need. We have to stop signing features off on technicalities."

Caroline: "Ok, but what do we do in the meantime? If we are taking a step back while we wait for requirements and design to catch up, what do the scrum teams work on?"

Cheryl: "Can you please go through the backlog and identify quick wins: small(ish) items that are ready for sprint that could fill the gaps while we wait for our top ten priority list?"

Caroline: "Well, there is always tech debt to tackle. Between that and little changes, I can keep them busy during sprint 5 and 6 at least."

Cheryl: "Ok, and in the meantime, Ulrich and Sara need to keep progressing the dashboard design as time allows. This is not carte blanche to down tools."

Caroline: "Understood. What are the next steps for agreeing on the top ten."

Cheryl: "This group gets back together a week from today to go through the proposal. I expect to see justification of decisions and want to understand the rationale for each. That means documenting the business outcomes that will result from building or not building each feature in detail."

Caroline: "And, how do I respond when I am getting pressure from John and the senior leadership team to keep delivering?"

Cheryl: "I'll talk to him. He wants the same thing we do. He'll understand."

Right, ok, fine. I'm oversimplifying. I admit it. But what the dialogue conveys is that strong leaders halt unproductive loops. Cheryl recognizes that the design team is on a hamster wheel that leads to nowhere without an emergency stop button. By calling this out and giving the team time to step back and take a breath, she will drive better development.

Negative loops must be broken: the team gets behind due to an unexpectedly complicated feature, unexpected vacancies or illness in the team, or any other of a number of valid reasons why they couldn't spend the time they needed on detailed designs. They try to make up for it by rushing through other designs. Those half-baked designs go into sprint, and as the design team is trying to move on to the next feature, they can't. They are pulled back into unpicking issues arising from the fact that the design they marked as done wasn't properly completed. I'm picking on the design team in this example, but this happens with requirements as well. If a product owner has an incentive just to get a feature done, rather than to get a feature right, you will end up with half-baked features.

# How to Break Negative Loops

Unpicking these issues cannot usually be accomplished in a single workshop, but you can minimize the incidences of half-baked feature design and requirements by doing a few things:

1. **Be a safe space for whistleblowers.** When team members have concerns about being overworked or seeing things go into sprint that aren't ready, encourage them to say something. And when they say something, address it. If you ask people to speak up, you have to listen.

2. **Focus on business outcomes, not inputs.** Who cares how many features a team completes if they are all terrible? No one. If team performance is measured on volumes of features delivered, you are incentivizing the wrong behavior. Yes, it takes longer to ensure that each major feature build has metrics that prove it accomplishes what it set out to accomplish, but it is worth it. Forcing the conversation has value, too. If the team cannot articulate what a feature is designed to accomplish, you should ask the team why they are building it.

3.  **Don't be afraid to slow down.** Your leadership
    team may not want to hear it, but taking the time to
    lay a good foundation pays dividends over the long
    term. Papering over early transgressions will not
    lead to a long happy career. Have the confidence
    and competence to be honest about what is working
    well and what isn't working well. If the team needs
    to slow down to restore balance, then slow down.
    Get the fundamentals right. No team ever won a
    championship by simply adding more trick plays
    and ignoring the fundamentals.

# Choosing the Right Features

It is imperative that teams show good judgment and the ability to make
sound, thoughtful decisions. Software development resources are
precious. They should be spent carefully. Lean-Agile principles were not
designed for this type of decision-making. They fall over in the face of
chunky corporate constraints. A chunky corporate isn't searching for new
features that will help it capture a customer base. Rather, it has a large,
mature customer base screaming for more features than it has resources to
deliver.

Cheryl must first document all of the features the team believe
they should build. This is probably where the list of fifty enhancements
originated. It started as two hundred product requests, but the product
team, using general intuition, whittled it down to fifty. The problem is
that fifty features over a six-month period is still too many. I've seen lots of
project plans reverse engineered from the number of features identified,
the amount of development resource and time allocated to the project,
and the project manager's gut feel as to whether the features are small,

medium, or large in build size. In these scenarios, the number of sprints assigned to each feature is a function of how many features need to be built rather than a function of how much time it would take to build each feature well. By doing this, we set our teams up for failure. Instead, a chunky corporate needs to get brutal when it approves enhancements. Priorities need to be tightly aligned to the aims of the business and agreed with senior leadership.

Once a list of features is compiled, Cheryl's team needs to determine which of these offer the greatest benefit to the business. These are not easy decisions. If they were easy, software projects would never run long, and customers would always be happy. Cheryl is deciding between two features: her clients want both of them. If she only chooses one, someone is going to be disappointed. She has resource to make one feature well. She must realize it is a choice between making one customer happy or making two customers unhappy with two poorly delivered features. This is the core value good product people bring to your business. If your product team members are not capable of making sound decisions when faced with difficult trade-offs, then you need to invest in up-skilling the product team. These very important decisions should not be made in a vacuum or a black box. They have substantial implications for the success of Acme's business. So how can you ensure the team is making thoughtful, informed decisions?

Create a scoring framework to enable thoughtful, informed decisions in a replatforming project. This gives team members a standard way of assessing the value of each feature, enabling comparison. A template helps ensure product managers and product owners value the features in a consistent way. I am using the word feature to represent enhancements. Some will be one feature, some will be multiple features. They do not correspond to singular features as described in a DevOps process. They more likely equate to epics, or groups of epics. The scoring framework begins with a set of questions and is summarized in Figure 5-3.

# 1. Does This Feature Already Exist in a Legacy Platform That's Being Replaced?

If so, give it a point. There will be customers that expect this feature to be delivered, and not delivering it may put customer migrations at risk. If no, award no points.

# 2. Is This Something That Is Used Frequently by Customers?

If so, award points proportionate to the amount of usage. If one hundred percent of customers use this feature, award 10 points. If ten percent of customers use it, award 1 point. If it is not used by customers, award no points. If this feature doesn't exist on your legacy platform, research whether or not competitors offer the feature. If they do, estimate how successful it is by asking your salespeople if prospective customers have mentioned it. You can also ask your existing customers if they are aware or interested in the feature. If competitors offer the feature and it seems in high demand, award a maximum of 5 points.

# 3. Do Customers Pay Separately for This Feature?

If yes, award points proportionate to how much customers pay. If they pay a lot, award 10 points. If they pay a little, award 5 points. If customers do not pay separately for this feature, do you have evidence that they would? If you have no evidence customers would pay separately for this feature, award no points. When making these sorts of difficult decisions, it is worth remembering that there is a correlation between the features offering the greatest benefit to customers and the features offering the greatest benefit to the business, but they are not necessarily the same thing. The likelihood that a customer will use a feature is important. However, the likelihood that a customer will spend money on a feature is also important. Therefore, propensity to spend money on a feature should be valued as well as the propensity to use a feature.

# 4. Is This Feature Aligned to the Product Value?

Does this feature sit naturally within the value proposition of the overall product stack? Or is it a "left-fielder"? Some features get built because a persuasive customer (or a customer willing to pay for a random feature) convinced the product team it would be just wonderful if the feature existed. That doesn't mean that the feature is in line with the overall value proposition that the platform delivers. It doesn't mean you should rebuild the feature, just because it exists today. If the feature is aligned to the product value, award 5 points. If not, award no points.

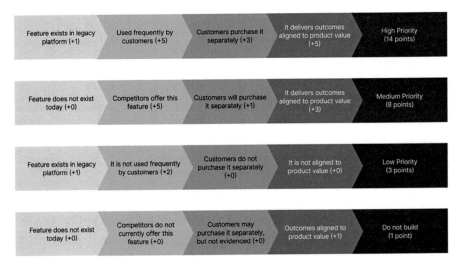

***Figure 5-3.*** *Sample product feature decision matrix*

Scoring individual features is an important part of the process, but it cannot be the only procedure a team undertakes to determine which features are important. There will inevitably be exceptions. A scoring framework is a good starting point, but no scoring mechanism is perfect. The scoring framework should be the baseline around which Cheryl's team debate the features that make it into the top ten. Over it, common sense should be applied. The scoring framework prompts product managers to conduct strong feature research. It should facilitate thoughtful debate about priorities. If product managers cannot answer the four questions listed above, then the team do not have enough information to make good decisions. They need tools and resources to score features accordingly.

Once features are scored, the scored list should be an easy way to separate out the strong contenders from the weak ones, but it should by no means be the only mechanism for making these decisions. Cheryl's team need to take a step back and check the numbers to see if anything looks out of place. Is there a critical feature that didn't score well but the team agrees needs to be rebuilt? Ok, how can the team rebuild it in a way that makes it more valuable? Is there a feature that scored well but feels like it will be obsolete soon? Ok, make a plan to speak with customers about whether or not this feature should be reimagined or put out to pasture.

Once the list is agreed, there should be very strict parameters around what constitutes a possible exception or change to the priority list. Scope creep refers to the expansion of a feature after it has been defined and agreed. Avoiding scope creep is critical to delivering features close to an agreed timeline. However, life happens, and there will be times when a new feature request supersedes all others. The difference between items that are derailing your project timeline from those that are speed bumps that you can manage appropriately will come down to how well communication is managed. If relevant stakeholders agree to put some features on hold in order to deliver a newly identified feature, that is fine. In fact, it should be expected.

Agility in the process is a good thing. However, when change is agreed, all stakeholders must be appropriately informed. It isn't the change that puts users' noses out of joint. Not being told about a change to the scope or the timeline, however, is incredibly frustrating for emotionally invested stakeholders. Appropriate management of expectations can be the difference between harmonious partnership and frustrated tension.

Cheryl must ensure there are appropriate processes in place to keep her team focused on what is agreed. What happens all too often is that market signals prompt a team to add a newly identified feature, but they don't take anything else *off* the plan to make room for the new feature. This is how roadmaps get overstuffed and previously reasonable timelines become unrealistic. This is why Agile roadmaps aren't supposed to have timelines: the aim is to enable this flexibility. Chunky corporate roadmaps have timelines, though, so this luxury must be sacrificed. When a new feature is introduced, stakeholders must have a forum in which they can ask the question: What are we going to stop doing to enable us to do this new thing?

# Existing Customers

Let's start by defining customers. Product and technology teams serve external and internal customers. When I talk about customers in this context, I mean both. Product professionals balance demand for features that serve internal customers alongside demand for features that serve external customers. Internal features include back office functions like subscription management, customer relationship management (CRM) integrations, marketing, and financial reporting. External features include enhancements to existing products and new products. When we talk about customers in this chapter, we mean both, and we recognize there will be tension between the priorities of the two groups.

Acme is struggling to prioritize a range of feature enhancement requests. The first thing Acme needs to define is whether it wants to be customer-driven or product-led. Blake says both. Yikes. How can Acme be both? Who decides what John's software development teams will build? Do customers decide? Or does the product team decide? If Blake thinks both can lead product decision-making, he asks the impossible of his product team. His desire to please customers limits the power of the product team to exercise product discipline. Without discipline, Acme struggles to deliver a scalable product stack.

Katie: "Blake, why are you spending so much money on a product team?"

Blake: "Come again?"

Katie: "Well, if your customers are making all the product decisions, what's the point? Why not save the money and eliminate the product department altogether?"

Blake: "I don't think I ever said customers get to make all the product decisions. All I ever said was we aim to be a *customer-driven* organization. I stand by that."

Katie: "You want your customers to drive."

Blake: "Yes."

Katie: "Are they good drivers?"

Blake: "What?"

Katie: "Does Acme's customer base know how to drive a product road map?"

Blake: "Come on. That isn't what I mean."

Katie: "What *do* you mean? If I don't get it, why do you think thousands of Acme colleagues across the business understand what you mean when you say *customer-driven*? You are telling colleagues to hand the keys over to customers and let customers drive them somewhere."

Blake: "I mean, not literally."

Katie: "How many customers does Acme have worldwide – like how many individual users?"

Blake: "About a million."

Katie: "You think those million individuals all want to go to the same place? Do you think they will all make sound decisions when choosing the best way to get to where they want to go?"

Blake: "Well, no, of course not. Product has to guide it – you know, decide which features we will build and which ones we won't and all that. But I want us to stay focused on meeting customer needs."

Katie: "You don't want Acme to be customer-driven. You want Acme to be customer-focused. There is a big difference."

It's about control and expectations. Being customer-driven, in contrast to being customer-focused, suggests that the business will do whatever customers want. That is madness at a chunky corporate. If customers are *driving*, they have the control. But they may very well crash the car. Put a million unlicensed drivers on the road – that's a recipe for bumper cars. And at the risk of being pedantic, I must point out that bumper cars don't go anywhere – they just spin in circles.

However, in a customer-focused organization, Acme can remain focused on three things that should guide feature decisions: (1) the problems the customer base solves with Acme software, (2) the features that appropriately balance expenditure with revenue generation, and (3) the features that provide Pareto optimal solutions for both Acme and its core paying customers.

Acme runs the risk of cutting its product function off at the knees through a poor choice of words. Blake is giving his sales and customer success colleagues free rein to promise anything and everything to its customers. He is setting Acme's technology team up for failure. Why would he put unproven, uninformed non-experts in charge of making product decisions that will determine the success and failure of Acme's business? Being customer-focused means Acme's customers tell it where they want to go, and Acme tells them whether or not it can take them there. If the answer is yes, Acme is in the driver seat. Acme determines the best route to get there. That is the difference. Product should be driving, not a passenger.

Good product managers are active leaders who determine which features will be built. When an organization is product-led, product managers are empowered to ensure software features are aligned to the strategic vision of the business. Sticking with the journey example, you can think of the strategic vision like a region. Our business will operate in London. Team, you have the freedom to make decisions about where in London you will go, but you must stay in London.

The product team operate like Black Cab drivers, seeing lots of jobs popping up: people on the street raising an arm, jobs via app – there are more requests for service than they can accommodate. They pick the jobs that are aligned to their region, ferrying customers around within London. Even within London, product managers will have to decide which jobs to take, and how to get from point A to point B.

Black Cab drivers in London have to complete something called "The Knowledge." It was first introduced in 1865, but what needs to be learned largely remains the same. Drivers must memorize all the roads and landmarks within a six-mile radius of Charing Cross. This amounts to around 25,000 streets. Naturally, GPS has changed dramatically the competitive landscape of taxi offerings in London, but I've still seen an experienced Black Cab driver outperform Waze or Google Maps. If a Black Cab driver says, "Maps is saying to take Tottenham Court Road, but I am not going near that this time of day; traffic is about to get a whole lot worse with the construction up there – they are opening and closing lanes multiple times a day – and by the time the traffic is reflected in the app, we'll be stuck," I listen.

I don't know if he is right or he is wrong, but I trust him. He has deep knowledge, confidence, and credibility. A Black Cab driver is better than his customer at predicting future traffic and knows the best route to take based on his experience. Technology helps, but it is supplemented by deep expertise. The passenger says where she wants to go, and the driver takes her there based on what he knows about the best way to get from point A to point B. That is what you want to foster in your product team to have a truly product-led business.

The best product managers are wise, decisive, and confident. The customer tells you where she wants to go. You tell her how you are going to get her there informed by a deep understanding of the technology landscape and priorities of the business. You might just be honest enough to say, "Hey, you are better off walking this time of day. It's only a ten-minute walk. If you get in the cab, you'll spend a pretty penny to sit in traffic for forty-five minutes." Product-led businesses know when a customer request will take them away from the strategic focus of the business or isn't worth the investment required from the customer to make it profitable.

Acme's product team should select scalable, repeatable product features that drive commercial success and meet customer needs. Individual customers have no incentive to pursue those objectives. Acme must be simultaneously product-led and customer-focused. A lean startup is trying to find market demand. A chunky corporate already has it. Acme should be listening to its customers. Product teams must understand at a detailed level what customers are trying to achieve in their daily workflows. A successful product team has the confidence and skills to identify what a customer wants to achieve and separate that from what a customer wants the software to do. Most customers make this hard for product professionals by providing feedback about how they want the software to work rather than what they want to accomplish by using the software.

Let's look at an example. Tricia is a customer of Acme Corporation. She works in finance and manages environmental reporting for Trees to You, a company selling seedlings to retail nurseries. Acme's Survey Division provides the software that helps Tricia to send online surveys to her suppliers for the purpose of collecting information on their carbon footprint. She uses responses to these surveys to complete her annual reports.

Tricia has noticed that the software automatically emails the Primary Business Contact (PBC) at the supplier company. Tricia asks her account manager at Acme, Janice, if they could develop a new feature to override the PBC selection and let her manually input email addresses. Janice puts Tricia in touch with a product manager, Taylor, who meets Tricia and asks about her request. Tricia says, "Can you just add a tick box here in the user interface where I choose to override the PBC email address and type in a new one?" Taylor scratches his chin. He immediately feels worried about what she is asking. He knows that free text entry of email addresses is a terrible idea: What if Tricia types the email address in wrong? The survey request could get lost. Tricia will not be any better off in this scenario. Many other customers may end up worse off as a result.

What will Taylor do? Well, if Taylor has been indoctrinated to be customer-driven, he is likely to say, "Yes, Tricia, we can do that. It isn't hard to change the code to add a tick box and a free text field." If Taylor has been trained to recognize that his value is in understanding of best practice in building software and managing data, he will have the confidence to think about the problem Tricia is trying to solve, rather than say yes immediately to whatever she is asking him to do.

Taylor responds by saying, "Thanks, Tricia, I understand you want to override the PBC data field with a new email address. Is the auto-populated email address from the primary business contact causing you problems?" Tricia responds: "Well, the last three months I've been chasing Highfield Nurseries to respond to my survey, thinking they were dodging me, but then I found out the PBC has been on maternity leave, and no one had received the survey request. As soon as we figured that out, they completed it. So, I need a way to change who the survey goes to, or to send it to multiple people."

Taylor says, "Ahh, I see, is it common that the primary business contact is not available at times? I imagine something similar would happen if that person goes on holiday or leaves the company without giving you a new contact."

Tricia: "Yes, exactly. This isn't the first time we've had delays in getting surveys returned because they weren't getting to the right people."

Taylor: "Ok, well, I wouldn't recommend we make that a free text field, as we will open up the possibility of typos or entry errors. However, we can look at a solution whereby you could add another email address from the list of contacts for the business. We have access to that data in the database."

Tricia: "Right, I get your point. Yes, that would work as a solution as well."

Taylor: "Ok, let me talk to the team and see if we can fit this in our planned product roadmap. I'll come back to you in the next couple of weeks and let you know where it sits on the priority list and if it is something we think we can accommodate. If so, I will let you know roughly when we would be able to look at it. At that point, I'll schedule some time with you again to talk in more detail about what the design team thinks would work best, and to make sure that will solve your problem. If the team don't have the capacity to work on it in the near future, I'll let you know that, too, and we can talk about possible workarounds to help you address the issue in the meantime."

In this scenario, Taylor is responsive to the problem Tricia is trying to solve but doesn't let Tricia dictate how it will be addressed. He stops short of promising it will be done or providing Tricia with a timeline that he may find later is unrealistic. However, he does commit to keeping Tricia informed on what the team can or cannot deliver. He is focused on solving Tricia's problem while acutely aware of the constraints the development team faces. He recognizes that setting unrealistic expectations for delivery with Tricia will do more damage to the relationship than being up front with Tricia that the team may or may not be able to deliver the improvements she wants in the near future.

Taylor maintains disciplined control of the product roadmap. He is also focused on customer satisfaction and solving Tricia's problem. He gives Tricia the attention she needs but does not let her dictate Acme's response. He is transparent about Acme's priorities and commits to having a follow-up conversation with Tricia to let her know the outcome of his investigation.

# Balancing Tensions Between Internal and External Customers

When time gets tight, a natural inclination is to postpone or put on hold the features that are for the use of internal customers. Internal customers are easier to disappoint. Usually, product teams justify this by agreeing with their business stakeholders that "it is only for a short time. We'll build it just as soon as we can." This creates tension between internal stakeholders in a business. Product teams should not ignore the internal needs of the business for the sake of customer features. They should manage decision-making regarding feature priorities in the same way, regardless as to whether the customer is internal or external and prioritize the roadmap as a whole based on the positive impact each feature will have. Features should be given priority when they deliver the largest benefit for the lowest cost. Software development for internal customers is more likely to be focused on reducing cost than driving increased revenue. Both deliver improved profitability.

Product managers tend to overestimate future revenue performance of new products. Cost improvements and productivity gains associated with automating internal processes, on the other hand, are often underestimated. For this reason, we observe a general bias toward features for external customers. For a chunky corporate seeking predictable performance, internal features, in many cases, are the safer play. Internal stakeholders can, if appropriately involved, carefully guide software development to ensure business objectives are met. Estimates of cost savings can be easier to calculate as compared to estimates of future sales. They depend on fewer uncontrollable variables, like sales focus and unknown market demand.

As an example, let's look at one of the most commonly automated back office functions: subscription management and customer billing. Caroline, Head of Development for Acme's Analytics Division, assigns her best product owner, Mo, to the job of managing subscriptions in the platform, or "subs and billing."

She warns him, "Subs and billing in a multi-national platform is one of the most complicated things I've ever worked on. Different countries have different rules for how tax is paid and how invoices are handled. Many countries require invoices to be filed with the government, and some countries even require that invoices filed with the government are sequenced in a certain way."

Mo: "Yikes."

Caroline (chuckling): "Don't worry," she says, "Luke is giving us two full-time finance people that will be embedded in the project until it is done."

Mo: "And Luke is cool with that? It sounds expensive for him."

Caroline: "Well, I strongly impressed upon him that he will unlock significant efficiency and be able to serve many more customers in the future with a lot less stress if we automate some of the processes his team members are currently handling manually. So, Jenna and Liam will be joining our cross-functional design team next week from finance. Team Apollo, headed up by scrum master Ylermi, is your assigned team. They'll work with you throughout. We expect the development to take at least six sprints."

Caroline recognizes it is not feasible to expect Mo to have a handle on the detailed financial requirements for Analytics Division's subscription and billing feature set. So, Jenna, Liam, and Mo work closely together over the next several months, designing new financial workflows, guiding engineers, managing third-party software plugins, and configuring back office workflows within them. This is cross-team collaboration at its best. When Mo has a question about how billing should work, Jenna and Liam respond almost instantly with informed advice about what the finance team needs. Mo, incidentally, sits next to another product owner working on the project, Carmen. She covers satellite imagery products.

In contrast to Mo's experience, Carmen is constantly complaining that when she has to ask the analysts a question about satellite images, they take ages to get back to her. Just last week she had a question from the engineering team. They wanted to know if the satellite images should load in portrait or landscape orientation by default. Carmen had to wait five days before she could get time in the diary of the three imagery analysts who could answer the question. That meant five days of the imagery scrum team paused while they awaited an answer on image orientation. Sure, they filled the time with other little jobs, but the planned feature delivery slipped into the next sprint. That, right there, is how inefficiency creeps into a software project. Hundreds of little delays add up to months of development time over the course of a large project. But I digress.

Back to Mo: when the new subs and billing system goes live, it isn't perfect, but it is a huge step forward for the finance team. The financial workflows in the platform are the most well-executed of all the elements of the new platform. When the kinks are worked out, and everything is running smoothly for subs and billing, Analytics Division is more efficient. They have laid a foundation that can support more customers with the same amount of resources in finance. If you want to make a feature build effective, you need to dedicate knowledgeable resources from across the business to it. It isn't enough for business stakeholders to provide input when requirements are being defined.

Questions will come up throughout the build process. The stronger the relationships between the engineers, product owners, and the internal customers they serve, the more efficient the build will be. When Mo and Ylermi have suggestions to improve financial workflows based on what they see in the application, they can workshop those ideas with Jenna and Liam. They can innovate collaboratively on process improvement, as they are coding. After sitting next to Carmen for a few months, Mo sincerely appreciates the time commitment from Jenna and Liam. He recognizes that strong, daily collaboration – not just within the scrum, but across a wider squad of stakeholders – is the difference between efficient delivery and delays.

Communication flows much more freely across strong relationships. The stronger the relationships between colleagues and the customer base, the more likely the engineering team is to understand what to build. It sounds pretty basic, but it is critical for the individual engineers who are writing the code have a deep understanding of why they are being asked to build an application, how the application fits into the platform, and what that software system is designed to do. A lean startup will probably only have one or two development teams. Business leaders, salespeople, and engineers will talk regularly, simply because there isn't anyone else to talk to, and business leaders and salespeople will double up as product owners, directing feedback on how features are working and how they could be improved. As a result of close collaboration, engineers are highly likely to have a deep understanding of what they are building, how it will be used, and the problems the platform aims to solve. Leaders drive effective cross-functional collaboration, regardless of organization size. It isn't rocket science. Delivering predictable performance is about executing the fundamentals well.

# Key Takeaways

- In a chunky corporate, the scope of enhancement requests is greater than the capacity to build them.

- Effective collaboration relies on relationships between stakeholders who work across reporting lines. Focus on building information flows across silos, not up and down them.

- Critical decisions about what features to build and how they are designed are made daily by these stakeholders. Give them the head space and resources to make good choices.

- You should be customer-focused but product-driven.

# CHAPTER 6

# The Challenges of Replatforming

Research from Forrester[1] indicates that "key performance indicators (KPIs) take a hit after a replatform goes live: 39% of companies surveyed reported their conversion rates were negatively affected after a new platform was launched." New sales and renewals are negatively impacted by replatforming in a significant number of replatforming exercises. That is a pretty big deal and a hidden risk most businesses do not expect nor actively mitigate. Replatforming is something most mature organizations will experience, but few do well. It will completely hijack the product roadmap and take up the bulk of development resources for a significant period of time. Maintaining and adapting products to respond to lean disruptors in the market while curating the existing book of business strains any product roadmap. This is a common source of tension between an organization's leadership team and its investor base. Managing this tension and replatforming well are critical because chunky corporates operate in relatively short investment cycles. Most investors – particularly for publicly traded or private equity-owned organizations – are focused on short-term performance. PE bought Acme two years ago. Replatforming Acme's core product stack will probably take five years. It is likely that

---

[1] "A Product Manager's Guide to Replatforming," January 22, 2018. www.mindtheproduct.com/product-managers-guide-replatforming/.

K. Tamblin, *The Lean-Agile Dilemma*, https://doi.org/10.1007/979-8-8688-0321-5_6

when Acme's investors are looking to sell the company, it will have just launched a number of replacement platforms. Acme cannot afford to take a revenue hit at the point PE wants to sell them. Therefore, immense pressure will be placed on Acme to demonstrate improvements in conversion rates and renewals as a result of the new platforms. And yet, thirty-nine percent of the time, the opposite happens.

So, what does this mean if you are a chunky corporate, with an aging fragmented set of platforms under pressure from newer, more modern products that were built less than five years ago? Well, if you are lucky, you will have the cash and margin capacity to invest in replatforming. Most projects start out something like this:

Chief Technology Officer (John), to his CEO, Blake, and the Board Chairman, Don: "We need to update our platforms in the Survey Division."

Don: "How much will it cost? How long will it take? How much additional revenue will it generate?"

John (*if he was speaking honestly*): "Probably $50 million, about five years, and impossible to say – it is more likely to prevent revenue loss than drive dramatically different revenue growth."

I mean, that just doesn't sound very good, does it? If you are an investor looking to exit your investment in three to five years, a five-year expensive software project that only pays off over a longer time horizon and has a very vague measure of its return on investment is not a logical thing to which you would agree.

Don: "No."

John: "Please?"

Don: "Come back with a business case that gets it down to $10 million, delivers in under two years, and drives two percentage points of incremental revenue growth, and we'll talk."

From that point forward, you are working with a restricted set of inputs rather than an outcome-focused plan. Under these conditions, it is very easy to forget what you are trying to accomplish. The *what* becomes generalist replatforming, and at this very point, you start to separate the project from the customer need. The project should start with the question: "What is the problem the platform solves? How could a new platform better solve that problem for existing customers and enable us to capture new customers?" A robust business case should start with the answers to those questions and layer in the cost and time estimates associated with delivering them. If that business case doesn't work financially, the team should go back to the drawing board. In Acme's case, though, Don has already sketched an outline of the business case without any regard to the problems it is trying to solve. John feels trapped and has no choice but to start working on a new business case with budget and timeline defined.

Every business case is wrong. Let's start there. I've never, in all my years of economic and business forecasting, seen a completely accurate forecast of multi-year costs, revenue, or profit. But that sure doesn't stop us as a profession from being completely obsessed with forecasting. And, yes, forecasting is incredibly important, but what is equally important is understanding the confidence interval around that forecast. What is the margin of error, and how does that margin of error build over time? Most confidence intervals around a forecast look like a Thanksgiving cornucopia (and the fat end is the margin of error around the ending point of your forecast). The further into the future you are forecasting, the less accurate your numbers.

So, what does that mean for the business case we are building to support the replatforming of our software? The success or failure of the project will depend on the success criteria as you define them in the beginning and the magnitude by which you miss your cost and revenue estimates. It isn't about whether your business case is right; it will be wrong, as we have established. The key to a forecast being useful is understanding at a substantial level of detail the levers that drive it, so the organization can determine proactively when it is going very wrong in a negative direction. Correlated to success is the ability to pivot at the earliest opportunity when signs suggest things are not going as planned.

The projects that are allowed to continue – either because project leaders cannot see or won't admit that things aren't going to plan early on – are the projects that become money pits. Even more worrying scenarios result when leaders can see it is going wrong but are impotent in efforts to get the project back on track.

John agrees to Don's terms. He knows it is the only way to upgrade Survey Division's software. The business case has been built; the investors have agreed; the money has been raised, borrowed, or stolen (well, hopefully not stolen). John is embarking on a replatforming exercise with the financial constraints outlined by Don. John and Blake now have a fixed amount of time in which to deliver a new platform. Existing customers must be migrated from the legacy Survey Division web platform to a new one. New software must replace old software. Right. Sounds obvious. But let's take a look at some of the less obvious implications of a replatforming exercise by comparing it to building a new product.

# The Challenges of Rebuilding a Legacy Platform

1. **Data.** Legacy platforms have more data than new platforms. Replacing a legacy platform requires migrating data.

2. **No MVP.** It's hard to release an MVP to customers when they already have a fully functioning platform.

3. **Obsolete features.** Legacy platforms have many more features than new platforms. Some of these should be eliminated to keep the software focused and manageable.

4.  **Roadmap.** The product roadmap is defined. If new features are added based on customer usage of an MVP, existing features will not be built, and the project timeline will change.

5.  **Managing change.** Customers don't like change. Delivering a seamless transition from legacy platform to new is really important but nearly impossible.

As customers use a software platform, data are created. If collecting information is a primary function of the software, data will be created and stored purposefully. Data could also come from how users interact with the software as usage statistics. Most new applications start generating data when the software goes live (or shortly before that). If the software has been in operation for a long time, existing data sets in the legacy platform (or legacy platforms, as the case often is) might be extremely large and sophisticated. The data sets will need to be extracted, cleansed, and migrated to a new location with a structure supporting the new design. Customers don't like losing their data when moving from an old platform to a new one, so whatever you do, don't throw away valuable data simply because it is stuck in a legacy platform.

I have worked with chunky corporates that have grown through acquisition, and chunky corporates that have grown organically. In both cases, legacy data sets are tricky to manage. They almost never rely on the same data structure. That means aligning them represents a great deal of work. This work is usually underestimated by technology and product-focused resources. To bring data from multiple databases into a single new database underpinning a new platform, there will be a shocking amount of data science required.

A lean startup will build a tiny piece of software, release it to new customers, and from there work dynamically with those customers to determine how the software should evolve to meet their needs. In a replatforming exercise, the existing features are reviewed, and the chunky corporate must decide which features to rebuild, which features to change, and which features to eliminate ("sunset" is corporate speak for feature elimination). Then a plan is made to rebuild the features that have made the cut and to migrate existing customers from the legacy platform(s) on to the new platform. This requires careful management of expectations within the base of existing customers. Existing customers will typically not be willing to use the new software until all critical features are replaced like-for-like (recall the description of asking the Joneses to move into a house with just a living room).

The chunky corporate leadership team will expect customers to pay more for a new platform, even if that platform has fewer features than the old platform. Customers, on the other hand, expect to pay less for a new platform if it has fewer features. Customers may ask for a price reduction to reflect reduced functionality of the new platform. Most chunky corporate leadership teams would not find this acceptable, however, as the investment required to replatform represents a cost burden to the organization, even if those costs are capitalized. It only takes one significant and grumpy customer, wedded to a feature that is expected to be sunset, to disrupt a perfectly lovely customer migration plan.

A lean startup, on the other hand, will recruit interested users to come and try out a new platform while it is in development or shortly after the release of an MVP. As the software grows, the lean startup can add customers. These customers are typically open-minded and excited to try something new. Particularly in markets in which the need met by the lean startup's software is underserved, customers will be eager to learn how to solve a problem using this new software.

At a chunky corporate, customers are often already grumpy because the software they are using (legacy platform) has become outdated and slow and is starting to fall behind competitive offerings. Customers have ideas in their heads about how the new platform should work: it is usually exactly how the old platform works, just faster and better. Customers' default position is most often reluctance to change. They also quite rightly feel entitled to continue using the old platform until such time as the new platform can do everything the old platform can do.

Ideally, they want to seamlessly transition from the old platform to the new without effort. If features have changed, however, customers are going to need to put in some effort to update expectations and ways of working. There is a balance to strike between old and new functionality. This is the opportunity to remove obsolete features and spend more time on delivering efficient, modern features. It is critical that an organization with a long history eliminates obsolete features. Otherwise, the platform will become unwieldy. Keeping a platform focused reduces product fragmentation and enables an efficient product stack.

Lev, VP of Product for Survey Division, is replatforming. Survey Division products are delivered via a legacy platform, called Origin, and a recently acquired platform, called Evolution. The replatforming exercise will deliver a new platform to which both Origin and Evolution customers will be migrated. In the Origin platform search application, customers have the ability to filter a search based on company size: small, medium, or large. This is referred to as the SML filter. In the Evolution platform, there is no SML filter. Instead, users can filter by number of employees and revenue. The new search application, called Flex, integrates features found in the Origin and Evolution applications. Flex works like the Evolution platform, allowing users to select a combination of filters, including revenue and number of employees, rather than having a single SML filter. In preparation for the migration of customers from Origin to Flex, an account manager submits an enhancement request.

The request states that Origin users are critically dependent on the SML filter, which does not exist in the new application, Flex. Lev asks one of his product owners, Nadim, to look into this. Nadim concludes the SML filter is not optimal. Company size can be based on revenue and/ or number of employees, and different users classify companies as small, medium, or large in different ways. The Pareto optimal solution is to let users filter searches by revenue and number of employees separately. Nadim tests his hypothesis to see if the same search results can be achieved by either method. He concludes that providing flexibility to users is the best solution, enabling the new platform to serve all users with the least amount of search filters.

Nadim speaks to colleagues and customers regarding this proposition. Some are receptive, but others worry that a few important customers will not like this change. They want search filters to work the same way they always did in the Origin platform. They worry that customers will refuse to migrate to Flex. Nadim pulls data from Origin and Evolution platforms. He finds that the SML combined search filter is used in twenty percent of all searches in the Origin platform. In Origin, an SML combined search filter is the only method by which a user can filter on company size. However, in the Evolution platform, where the SML filter sits alongside individual filters for revenue and number of employees, the SML filter is only used one percent of the time.

Now Nadim has the numbers to validate his hypothesis that the SML filter is redundant in the face of individual filters for number of employees and revenue. It's not exact A/B testing, because the selection of customers isn't random, but it is a pretty darn close proxy for it. This method requires significantly less effort than building a proper A-B test. Armed with these metrics, Nadim works with concerned colleagues and customers to demonstrate how to achieve the business outcome they seek (identifying companies by size) without building a redundant software feature (an SML filter).

Once Lev knows which features must be sunset, it is imperative that the team communicate it to Survey Division's customers. Reaching alignment regarding what users will be asked to give up at the point of migration is imperative. If customers do not participate in the process of sunsetting old features, they will likely object. The more objections they raise, the less likely they are to move willingly from old platform to new. Survey Division then runs the risk of being held hostage to legacy customer demands. Blake does not want to find himself in a situation in which Acme is ready to migrate customers to the Flex Application, but some vocal customers refuse to migrate due to the loss of a search filter. There are simple steps Acme can take to minimize this risk.

The customer support team needs to give customers warning and time to get used to the idea of living without the SML filter. They need to be shown how they can accomplish the same thing with different filters as they exist in the Flex platform. Most won't have the time or patience to just figure that out on their own. Acme needs to manage the change with its customers proactively so that any workflows they have that depend on these features can be rebuilt in the new world.

Katie: "Once I worked on a project where we didn't give customers enough advance warning of some differences between the old and new platforms, and they ended up holding us hostage to the old features. We had to add back search filters we were confident would not be used simply because the customers refused to use the new platform until they had like-for-like features. A year later, we confirmed no one was using the redundant features they demanded. It was incredibly irritating and a huge waste of resources."

Blake: "Ok. I'll work with the product team to get a list of features being sunset. How do we get out in front of it?"

Katie: "In my experience, the best way to approach it as is if it were a machine part – like a product obsolescence process. You have a plane, right?"

Blake: "Of course I do. I am the CEO of a successful company, so my hobbies include flying my Cessna 172 on the weekends."

Katie: "You are a douchebag. But, putting that to one side, what happens when you need a replacement part that is no longer manufactured?"

Blake: "Oh, Christ, I get these emails all the time advising me of parts that will no longer be available after a certain date. I usually ignore them."

Katie: "But at least you were warned. And if you find that you can't get the replacement part you need when you need it?"

Blake: "Last time that happened, Cessna offered me a slightly larger assembly. I needed a gasket for a fuel indicator, but...."

Katie: "I am bored already."

Blake: "...But, they don't make the gasket anymore. So, they offered to sell me the whole fuel assembly instead. It costs a little more, but it worked. And, I couldn't get mad because they had sent me a notification about the gasket being discontinued like five years ago or something. I ignored their message."

Katie: "Well, that is my point. We need to proactively communicate to our customers that the SML filter will no longer be available in the new platform. We make it a deprecated feature – one that we advise against using so customers get used to living without it. Then we need a little video to show them how to use the filter for employees and the filter for revenue to create the same search result. And we need to tell them with advance warning, as they might have automated reports that run off of the SML filter that will have to be rewritten to work in the new system. We should offer to help them recreate them."

Blake: "Fair point. That should help ease the transition."

Katie: "It will make it more likely we can sunset the SML filter with minimal complaint or disruption to customers. It doesn't mean no one will complain, but we will have the tools to manage them when they do. Just like you and your gasket."

In contrast to customer preferences for a simple, like-for-like upgrade, product teams at chunky corporates usually want to add some flair to the new platform. They want to innovate and build new and better features. Replatforming is where the allure of building new products comes into conflict with the business objective. Customers and Board members want product managers to rebuild existing features, faster and better. Product people want to build new features and wow their customers with their brilliant ideas.

There are two very serious challenges with this tension between what product people want to do and what customers and the Board expect. First, if customers don't want to use the new platform until it is mature and can do everything the legacy platform could do, that means that the new platform is not likely to be tested by actual customers until very late in the build. Second, new platforms always have kinks to work out, and it is difficult to predict how many resources will be needed to work out those kinks. The longer the kinks have gone undetected in the build, the more complex they can become. If there is a kink in the core functionality of the platform, and features are built on top of the core functionality before the kink is discovered, you can find yourself with a whole lot of kinks to work out at the point you go live with customers.

Six months later, Blake has called a meeting together with his CEO of Survey Division, LaTonya, and his CTO, John. On the agenda is Survey Division's replatforming project, which is falling behind. Blake says to LaTonya, "Up until very recently, product was an invisible function to me." He goes on to explain that he had assumed that decisions about the product roadmap were made by business leaders that understood the competitive landscape, the needs of his customer base, and the vision for the business. He has just discovered, however, the development team has spent the majority of the last three months working on feedback from customers they asked to test Survey Division's MVP. In the meantime, the set of features that must be delivered before customers can be migrated to the new platform has been put to one side. The project is now three months behind schedule.

Blake cannot get a straight answer when he asks the team how that decision was made. He rolls his eyes and says, "If anyone explains Agile and Lean principles to me again, I am going to scream. What I want to understand is who is making the decisions about what we build and when? Why is that such a difficult question? And why have I never realized how much power lies in those decisions before?"

When customers use a legacy platform that has been in operation for years, most of the kinks have already been worked out. Over the years the legacy platform has been in use, bugs have been fixed, and new features have been added. Unless the team spend an equal amount of time building a new platform to replace the old one, the new platform will logically be less feature-rich and more prone to workflow gaps or bugs. Anytime you swap a mature platform, even a slow and ugly one, for a new platform, you will inevitably hit teething problems. New customers to a slick lean startup are quick to dismiss teething problems as all part of the new software experience. Customers of a chunky corporate, in contrast, will feel disgruntled if the new platform feels like a step backward in their user experience. They will swiftly start asking for discounts or threatening cancellation if teething problems are not addressed.

At this point, product and development teams are faced with a difficult decision: should we derail our replatforming project plan to put resources on working out teething issues, or do we stick to the replatforming project plan we shared with the Board because the Board have given us a set amount of time to deliver the project? If they go for the first, derailing the project plan to work out kinks, the Board will be upset. If they don't work out the kinks, customers will be upset. You'd be surprised how many companies, when faced with this scenario, choose to keep the Board happy and hope customers don't get so upset they leave.

Business leaders are usually hopeful they can address user experience issues before customers cancel. They also discount future risk of customer upset when faced with a very imminent risk of upsetting the Board by announcing a delay. Sometimes the people making these decisions talk to the Board more often than they talk to their own customers. Over time, customers grow more and more disgruntled. Once the customers go from disgruntled to upset, the team will have to scramble to stop kinks from turning into a customer retention issue.

Rebuilding a platform, as opposed to building a new one, raises unique challenges. As described, they stem from the inability to release an MVP to customers, the tensions raised by a governing board that expects fixed timelines, the complexity associated with managing existing data sets, and the unique incentives facing customers who already have working software and must be enticed or forced to change. These challenges are summarized in Table 6-1.

***Table 6-1.*** *Replatforming raises unique challenges not addressed by Lean-Agile principles*

|  | **Lean Startup** | **Chunky Corporate** |
| --- | --- | --- |
| Data | Non-existent or small | Large and siloed in multiple databases with different data models |
| MVP | Released to customers as soon as possible | Ignored by existing customers using a more feature-rich legacy platform |
| Obsolete features | Non-existent or small | Must be sunset |
| Roadmap | Feedback driven | Defined by features in legacy platform |
| Customers | New and excited | Resistant to change with high expectations |

# New Customers vs. Old Customers

I have seen a number of chunky corporates build a new platform and start onboarding new customers before migrating existing customers to it. Inevitably, when this approach is taken, the new platform sits alongside the legacy platform for years with the likelihood of ever migrating legacy customers reducing with each passing month. There are multiple natural reasons for this. The first is that new customers using the new platform start to ask for more functionality. In responding to those requests to keep the new customers happy, development teams get distracted from rebuilding the old features that exist in the legacy platform.

Why? New features are more exciting. They give the product team a greater opportunity to scratch the product design itch. Building new products is more fun than reimagining old ones. Old features awaiting rebuild in the new platform are left in the backlog. As a result, migrating old customers from the legacy platform to the new platform is delayed.

Eventually, the new platform diverges so much from the one it was trying to replace; migration of existing customers to it becomes virtually impossible (or, if not impossible, then at least undesirable).

Blake, Don, and I, as Board members of Acme Tech, once looked at a company under the auspice of potentially acquiring it. As part of this process, we evaluated all of the company's software products and the customer workflows they supported. We learned that the company was building a new platform, and their most recent customer wins were onboarded directly on to the new platform. They touted this as a great success and patted themselves on the back for adhering to Lean-Agile principles. They had built an MVP and had new customers using it. It was all very exciting. The new platform was great and getting amazing feedback from their new customers. And, yes, they reassured us, they were planning to migrate their existing customers on to the new platform.

This is where I became skeptical. The more we dug into the detail, the more we found that the new platform had overlapping features with the old platform. However, the data generated and used by these features were different. Many of the features in use by customers on the legacy platform weren't built yet in the new platform. They intended to run both platforms in parallel while they replaced all the features from the old platform in the new platform, they assured us.

*Red flag.* They had no evidence that the data from the old platform could be easily moved to the new platform, or that their legacy customers would agree to move to the new platform. They were on a path to product fragmentation. I was concerned that the two product roadmaps would continue to diverge, as newer customers on the new platform asked for different features from the old customers on the old platform. Over time, this widens the gulf between the two systems, making it harder and harder to migrate legacy customers from the old platform to the new one.

So, what they are likely to end up with is not a replacement platform but a new platform that is separate and distinct from the old. My fear: never the twain shall meet. I advised Blake and Don of my skepticism.

We did not acquire this company in the end, and, sure enough, when we checked in with them two years later, they still had two separate platforms running alongside each other. The data models of those two platforms would have diverged so significantly in those two years that I dread to think what gremlins they will find in the foundations when they are forced to sunset the old platform. Their replatforming exercise had failed. They successfully built a new product but failed to sunset the old. You can see how it happens rather more easily than one might think. They applied Lean-Agile principles without considering how their existing platform made Lean-Agile a poor methodology choice.

Here a chunky corporate finds itself in a Catch-22 of sorts: if it wants to get an early MVP out to real customers for testing, it should put new customers on the new platform, even before that platform reaches parity with the old platform. In doing so, it will create tension between the Lean-Agile principles of adjusting the build in response to early customer use of the platform and the features required to replace the old platform. If the chunky corporate decides not to onboard new users to the new platform until it reaches feature parity with the old, the existing features remain largely untested until the point existing customers migrate from the old platform to the new.

Thus emerges the replatforming dilemma: put new customers on the new platform or stay focused on migration? Unfortunately there is no right or wrong answer, but simply different elements to manage. If you put new customers on the platform before migrating old customers, you must exercise extreme discipline as those new users provide you feedback for improvement. You cannot allow that feedback to divert attention from the existing customer migration. If you focus on rebuilding existing features so you can migrate customers first, you must accept that your software will not be used by real customers until later in the process than Lean-Agile principles dictate. In this case, you must rigorously test your platform throughout the build.

# Is Your MVP a Major Validation Problem?

You can hardly fault the well-meaning chunky corporate that intends to migrate customers to the new platform eventually but gets distracted by the demands of new customers using the platform. Their hearts are in the right place. They envision a customer migration but are unable to execute it because the MVP takes on a life of its own. Avoiding this outcome, however, doesn't mean the organization can scrap the concept of an MVP altogether. It's still a darn good idea to release a small version of the software to testing as soon as possible. It is equally good practice to assume items will be missed in design and to leave room in the roadmap to deliver them. If getting features right is sacrificed to keep the project timeline intact, you will find yourself facing a Major Validation Problem: a platform full of half-baked features, none of which deliver the desired business outcomes.

Without customers to test feature sets as they are built, replatforming exercises rely on QA and internal business testers (usually volunteers) to identify bugs, design gaps, and areas for improvement. However, these issues are usually discovered when customers use a platform at scale, not by internal testers. Relying solely on internal testing across a complex platform leaves you with a Major Validation Problem. Blake and Tilen experience this when rolling out online payments for the Well-being platform, which offers a product line that works on an annual subscription. For years, most subscription payments were made by bank transfer.

When the Well-being platform is upgraded, the product team recommends improving the checkout process to include auto-renewal and online card payments to drive efficiency. The hypothesis is if more people renew automatically and pay online, Publishing Division will spend less account resource on chasing payment. So, time in the development road map is set aside to implement online payments. The product owner, Deena, writes up the user stories. They go into sprint. Auto-renewal and online payments go live in the system. However, issues start to come to light when Alfredo, the Finance Business Partner for the Publishing Division, approaches Tilen with a question.

Alfredo: "Tilen, we've got the first set of numbers back since we put card payments live in the system."

Tilen: "And?"

Alfredo: "Well, they are lower than we expected, to be honest."

Tilen: "How low?"

Alfredo: "We are only successfully getting companies signed up to automatic payment at renewal about thirty percent of the time."

Tilen: "What? Why?"

Alfredo: "I have no idea. I would have expected more like ninety percent."

Tilen contacts Blake and John to let them know there is an issue. John asks George, the Head of Development for Publishing, to look into it and then organizes a call with Tilen, George, Deena, and Alfredo. George invites the scrum master assigned to this feature, Damian, to the call.

Tilen: "Thanks, John, for organizing the call. What's going on with autopayments? Why is the uptake so low?"

John: "George, over to you."

George: "Yes, well, Damian and I looked into the issue. In order to successfully enroll a customer in autopay at the time of their renewal, we have to record a token that enables us to access their card details via our payment provider. Unfortunately, that token is not stored in three scenarios: (1) there is a discount applied to the order or (2) the company is tax exempt or (3) the company is paying with an international card. We encounter one of those scenarios about fifty percent of the time. That will drag the figures down."

Tilen: "Let me get this straight. We waited months to get autopayment live in the system and you are now telling me it only works fifty percent of the time? Why doesn't it work in those three scenarios?"

George: "You never asked for it to work in those three scenarios."

Ok, I'm gonna pause here for a minute, because Tilen's head is about to blow off. This aside is for any engineer, scrum master, or product owner reading this: If you ever find yourself tempted to tell a senior leader in your business that something doesn't work as they expected because someone failed to document all the scenarios in which it should work, stop yourself immediately. It may be true you weren't asked to cover these scenarios. It may be true that you had already moved on to work on some other high-pressure deliverable by the time the team figured out it didn't work.

However, neither of these truths will excuse you for not delivering the expected business outcome. Your senior leaders will not think better of you because it was someone else's responsibility to tell you what to build. Your senior leaders expect you – engineer, product owner, scrum master – to *think*. Senior leadership expects the technical expert in the room to highlight the fact that these scenarios were missed and to keep working on the feature until it meets the expected business outcome.

Tilen may say, "George, I think you are missing the point. It should have been pretty obvious to anyone taking the time to think through what we are trying to achieve that we need autopay to work for the majority of our customers, many of whom will have discounts, be tax exempt, or pay with international cards." Tilen, while saying the above, is thinking: *our tech team is in absolute shambles. How did NO ONE mention this major oversight in the design and development of what was meant to be a very important tool for the business?* Tilen reports to Blake that he can't get any more efficiency out of his renewals team because the tech built to support them is not sufficient. If we dig into these dynamics, what you see at play is the hierarchical silo in full operation. The boundary tech has drawn for itself is along the delivery to a requirement, not the delivery of a business outcome. In a lean startup, by contrast, there are no such silos: you either deliver the business outcome, or you go home.

Setting appropriate expectations of rework on an MVP is key. This oversight could have been picked up in an MVP for autopay if the first version of autopay was released with an MVP mindset. The team, Deena,

Damian, George, and Alfredo, need to see what happens when real users interact with the feature before moving on to something else. This is when the business hypothesis of a more efficient renewal and payment workflow is tested – not before. The feature should not be considered complete until the business outcome is delivered. If the team catches the design gap early, and Damian's scrum has space in its backlog to address the issues, they avoid the Major Validation Problem.

Sadly, though, the chunky corporate application of MVP has devolved into releasing just *a stripped-back version of what you really want*. That isn't a problem if the more complete version of what you want follows shortly after the MVP. However, chunky corporate software projects have long, defined product roadmaps, so, as soon as the MVP is released, so is the scrum team. They immediately move on to something else, leaving that shitty MVP as the de facto product feature.

This is a natural result of the scope of features needing to be built being greater than capacity available to deliver them in the timeline approved by the Board. In chunky corporate world, there is no space in the roadmap to iterate on an MVP and address what is missed in design. Therefore, most features in chunky corporate software end up half-baked upon release. They stay half-baked until stakeholders shout loudly enough to not be ignored. Chunky corporates are always trying to do too much in too small a timeframe (years' worth of software building condensed into six to twelve months of replatforming). Instead of delivering fifty half-baked features, chunky corporates should deliver ten well-developed features. Do less, but do it well. Your customers will prefer it.

Damian's scrum had two sprints to deliver autopay. He did what he could do in two sprints. He knew it was less than ideal. Deena, the product owner writing requirements, knew it was less than ideal. But they are under pressure to get working on something else as soon as possible. If Damian flags the oversight, he will miss his deadline. Damian tries to blame Deena, as she owns the task of writing requirements and she didn't explicitly outline requirements for these scenarios. Deena thinks Damian should have told her there were multiple scenarios in which it would fail. Probably no one could have foreseen that autopay would fail in those scenarios. But where chunky corporates get it wrong is in not giving Deena or Damian the space to put it right.

If Tilen is aware of the issue and the resources required to set it right, he, Blake, and John can make an informed decision about priorities. They can agree how and when to address it. But because Damian did not engage with business stakeholders when the gaps were identified, they stripped Tilen of the opportunity to make a judgment call. The low uptake in autopay isn't the result of a thoughtful decision among a group of stakeholders. It is the result of an insular group of development resources either hiding from what they knew would probably be a difficult conversation or blissfully unaware that what they built was inadequate. Technology and product leadership have not set the bar very high regarding the expectations of quality and completeness of what their teams deliver. If they let this one slide, they enable the half-baked mindset to establish itself in the business fabric.

Alternatively, if George and John approached the feature release with an MVP mindset, they could accept that the initial release of autopay would require rigorous testing from real users before the team could have any confidence regarding its completeness. Damian and Deena would have had not only the freedom but also an imperative to get it right before calling it done. Business stakeholders, including Tilen, would have had appropriate expectations regarding the additional sprints required to address gaps discovered when autopay goes live. It is optimistic – no, that isn't a strong enough word – it is *foolish* to think that any new software feature is going to be released in perfect working order.

The time pressure leadership teams put on their scrums to complete features and move on creates bad incentives. It incentivizes scrum teams to hide inadequacies, not iterate on them. It is where the MVP loses all meaning. Suddenly, because timelines are fixed and targets are ambitious, what was scoped as an MVP becomes the feature users have to live with for as long as they can. That is not a minimum viable product. That is a major validation problem waiting to happen.

# Key Takeaways

- Replatforming projects have set budgets and timelines agreed between investors and leadership. Pressure to successfully replatform within that agreement will be high as deviation from the project outline could negatively impact an investment cycle.

- When replatforming, your MVP is larger than the software you are replacing; it's more than minimum.

- Avoiding a major validation problem requires two things: (1) flex in the roadmap to address oversights when they are discovered and (2) rigorous early testing to catch design gaps or oversights early.

# CHAPTER 7

# Replatforming the Right Way

When undertaking a replatforming exercise, one must consider both the approach and the execution. We will look at each of these in turn, starting with the former. The approach to replatforming sets out a framework within which the project takes shape. If the approach is less than thoughtful, the project may be doomed from the start.

## Define the Vision

Why are you replatforming? There isn't much point in throwing out an old platform and replacing it with a new one that does exactly the same thing in exactly the same way. If you are replatforming, rather than just updating code, ask yourself, what are you trying to achieve? What do you need the new platform to do that the old one cannot? What obsolete features are no longer needed?

When you are replatforming, the *what* is relatively defined. You know the problems you are trying to solve for your customers; that should not change dramatically. If it does, you are not replatforming. In that case, you are building a new product line, and you will struggle to sunset the old one. The focus of your vision for replatforming should be on the *how*. How can you solve existing customer problems more efficiently and provide

K. Tamblin, *The Lean-Agile Dilemma*, https://doi.org/10.1007/979-8-8688-0321-5_7

a comfortable transition to the new platform? This is where chunky corporates should focus innovation efforts. Innovate on the *how*, not the *what*.

Defining the vision for a platform that will replace a previous product stack requires a mix of internal and external knowledge. Internal colleagues have valuable institutional knowledge about what has been tried in the past, what works for your customers, and what probably won't. But internal colleagues will also be biased toward the way things have always been done. That bias is often unrecognized, unintentional, and is the equivalent of putting blinders on a horse. It makes it very difficult to see the field. In this case, the *field* is the competitive and technological landscape of existing and emerging products. The team must understand not only the way things have been done in the past but also how things are done by competitors and how they could be done more efficiently.

You need to understand where your customers want to go. Where is the market headed? What foundational elements of the new platform are necessary to support customers? This is where external knowledge can help. Whether it is bringing in fresh eyes to look for new approaches to old problems, or whether it is engaging market experts to understand how disruptors are solving old problems in new ways, external expertise can help unlock innovation even when the *what* you need to build is defined.

It is important that external knowledge remains focused on the *how* and does not inadvertently change *what* the platform does for customers. Setting clear boundaries of the product and clearly defining the market space in which the product will operate are critical elements of the project design. What the software does, that is, the business problems it solves for customers, must remain consistent. How the software works, that is, how it solves those problems, is defined by the vision.

# Get the Data Right First

I have seen data issues add years, yes, you read that right, *years*, to more than half of the replatforming projects I've supported in my career. Development teams are so eager to get coding, they start building the software before data are aligned. Most leadership teams leave it to the CTO to set up, design, and kick off a software project. In this case, John, CTO of Acme Tech, does what most CTOs do. He gets the team designing and coding as quickly as possible. John has overlooked the critical difference between a lean startup and a chunky corporate, though. Acme has millions of data points in its existing platforms. Those data points are valuable to Acme's customers. They must be easily accessible in the new platform. John's team needs to move all of the data into a common format and location first. He should not start coding until this is done.

If the team writes software code based on an incomplete data set, or, even worse, without using real data to test the code, they will inevitably encounter problems when users attempt to access real data in the platform. Data are the foundation of the house. In building a house, digging the foundation is typically where you get surprised by extra time and cost requirements that the builders couldn't foresee. Builders who have a lot of experience are often quick to say, "Well, the project will take six months, and cost this much, if we don't find anything unexpected underground. But if we start digging and find issues with the soil or in laying the foundation, it might take an extra few months and cost you much more." I say the same things about data. Data are where many gremlins hide and data gremlins are extremely difficult to eliminate if the code is already written.

This is not an issue for most lean startups because they build the data set alongside the code. There are exceptions to this, of course. Some startups rely on vast existing data sets to deliver value for customers. Some spend years getting to know that data before building any front end product. But those exceptions aside, most lean startups can start coding quickly and figure out what the data looks like as they go along without causing too many problems. For chunky corporates like Acme, though, customer value is tied up in the data collected over the years its legacy platform has been operational. Data provide a strong product moat to other would-be entrants to the market.

How can you be sure that you've got the data right? It's simple: build the foundation before you build the house. Pull together the data you need to run your platform into a logical, structured set. That may be a data warehouse; it might be a data lake; it might be a knowledge graph; it might be a set of tables. Whatever it is, make sure existing data flow into it and the structure makes sense. Most projects start with a data model or data design. These are important assets, but they are not enough. It is equally important to see real data loaded into the new structure. The real data, whether a subset of the whole or not, needs to include data from all origin data sources covered by the project.

Lots of issues crop up when you dig into actual data, beyond the logical representations of the data. Don't get fooled into thinking that you are done when the data design and logical data model (LDM) are agreed. Real data in the warehouse will prove that the LDM works as a physical model, and you will likely need to adjust it multiple times to account for things that could not be foreseen. I've approved plenty of LDMs because they look sound on paper; however, when we started using actual data we found many elements that were not addressed by the LDM. As with anything, it is easy to see what is wrong in a LDM but virtually impossible to see what is missing. Only when you start to interact with actual data will you see what was previously overlooked.

A simple example of this is time zone. John approves the LDM for Survey Division's new platform that includes a time stamp when data are updated. It works fine when the software is used in the UK. But, as soon as the team rolls the platform out to Europe, they start recording bugs related to time stamps. European customers complain that all records of time are in Greenwich Mean Time (GMT). When the system sends them reminders for deadlines, customers in Central European Time (CET) receive them one hour too late. When users sign up for a survey, they are given a deadline to complete it. A reminder goes out at 11 p.m. on the day of the deadline. However, 11 p.m. GMT is midnight in CET, so users receive reminders at the time the deadline passed, not one hour before.

The question comes to Remi, Head of Delivery for Survey Division: "Why are time stamps not recorded in local time zones?" Remi doesn't know; he asks Corey, the Technical Architect. Corey responds, "There is no element in the database for time zone. There is no existing way to separately capture the time and the time zone. When a user signs up for the survey, the time is recorded directly, and the code assumes all users are in GMT. It's an oversight. When the team put the LDM together, they didn't think about the fact that someday there would be multiple time zones to manage."

By the time Remi reports the cause of time-related bugs to John, multiple features in the platform are operating on a simple twenty-four-hour clock that doesn't consider time zone. Instead, time zone has to be added first to the database and populated with values. Notifications and email templates must be updated to include time zone. The UI must be updated to show time zone. This silly little oversight costs Remi weeks in rework across the platform. Remi and John delay other feature releases in order to free up development time to manage time zone data. That gremlin could have been avoided if Remi and John had pulled data from across Europe and the UK (and the Americas and Asia) into the data set before the code was written. If the QA team tested the system using data from multiple time zones, they could have caught the issue early. Instead, the team put a house on a foundation that was missing several bricks.

# Design, Execute, and Check

Effective design within the context of a complex replatforming project requires detailed, multi-disciplinary planning. Why is it important that replatforming is a multi-disciplinary effort? Platforms at mature organizations provide services both to customers and back-office functions. Services support the workflows of internal and external users. Applications within the platform align to the processes of the people using them. Existing processes and procedures should be optimized in the design of the new platform.

However, as most chunky corporates scale, design resources are specialized and spread thinly across multiple scrum teams. Replatforming requires strong, sensible, thoughtful design to enable complex technology ecosystems to operate efficiently. Build architectural muscle early in the replatforming process, and give your technical design team the time and resources necessary to enable scalable designs that will effectively serve the future needs of the business.

Equally, when you have multiple teams working on a single platform at the same time, they can quickly lose a grip on exactly how the various elements of the platform are being coded. The sheer volume of code being generated in a large replatforming exercise makes it very difficult for technology leaders to read, check, or provide guidance across all of it. This is why detailed architectural design is so important. Engineers across the project must work to the same specification to ensure the applications knit together into a functioning platform. It is critical that technical designs cover all aspects of the build: data structure and storage, technical design, process workflows, user interface assets, NFRs, and more.

I've worked on multiple replatforming exercises in which the detailed architectural design called for micro-services, or lots of little applications that run separately but fit together seamlessly. However, when the platform started to scale, and problems emerged, we found that we did not have a platform made up of lots of micro-services, but a monolith.

Despite having a technical design asset that described separation of services, various scrum teams piled more and more code on to the same code base. While micro-services were referenced in the design documents, they were not executed appropriately. Managers weren't holding scrum teams to account or checking their work as they went. Now, it doesn't really matter whether you want to build micro-services or a monolith. What is important is that you build what you set out to build. When back-end design is not respected, performance of the user interface suffers.

If the picture of a little spinning wheel, or, depending on how old you are, an hourglass, just popped into your head, you are getting it. Load time. Pages within the platform should load instantly, with a maximum loading time of two seconds. If your page takes more than eight seconds to load, you have lost your user to another task. Trust me, when your users tell you that your platform is slow, brace yourself.

When performance issues arise, first you must understand if they are systemic or isolated. Hopefully, if they are isolated, and you catch them quickly, they are simple to address. Remember how we explained that replatforming can be a Major Validation Problem? A lot of interconnected services must work before customers migrate to the new platform. That limits the real-world testing undertaken before going live. Transitioning from a QA team testing a platform to hundreds or even thousands of real users overnight opens up the risk that systemic performance issues lurk across various pages and workflows. A non-performant application can be a can of worms: usually it is not one issue, but many. Getting to the root cause of systemic performance issues can eat up development resources and very quickly turn into a quagmire.

A strong design and carefully curated coding of that design mitigates the risk of performance issues and ensures the platform is built as it was intended, reducing the risk of having a Major Validation Problem. Design must go further than a pretty architectural drawing in PowerPoint. Teams must understand, in gross detail, how the applications fit together and what purpose each feature within each application serves, both architecturally and commercially. Design documentation should explicitly spell out which elements of the system are to be supported by software applications and what the boundaries of those applications will be. How services and applications fit together and what architectural and infrastructural artifacts are required must be explicitly outlined in the technical design.

Execution must be thorough. The definition of done should include both technical and commercial success criteria. Accountability for meeting these must rest on the shoulders of both product owners and scrum masters. Testing must check that execution has been successful in delivering end-to-end workflows that actually work. Test cases must include elements of technical infrastructure as well as user experience.

# Get Close to Your Colleagues and Customers

Gathering information from internal and external sources is critical to setting out the vision of your replacement platform. That doesn't end when the vision is defined. It is critically important that both your colleagues and your customers come on the journey from an old platform to a new platform with you as you build. The biggest enemy to a successful replatforming exercise is arrogance. It is arrogant to think that a single team can deliver a replacement platform.

A successful replatforming exercise relies on participation from across the organization. The last thing we want to do, which often ends up happening, is we build a new platform to support old processes. The reason this is such a common occurrence is simple: the people that could optimize the processes are not as intimately involved in the project as they should be. In order to take a multi-disciplinary approach, the design team must collaborate with stakeholders to understand how processes *could* and *should* be done, not just how they *are* done. Lean startups do not typically have sophisticated internal business processes, which explains why this challenge is not addressed appropriately in Lean-Agile principles. All too often, replatforming looks like a black box in which the technology team and the product team go away and do all sorts of magic to decide what to build and how to build it. To be successful, communication needs to continue throughout the process. No one likes a black box approach.

Avoiding the black box approach requires time from colleagues outside of technology, and that time commitment is not to be underestimated.

It is equally critical to leverage strong relationships with external customers. In a chunky corporate, teams must manage expectations accordingly. Telling a customer you are going to deliver a new platform on a specific timeline is dangerous. Projects notoriously run over predicted timelines, and, for some reason completely unbeknownst to me, it is not obvious to all that if the timeline for the project shifts, someone needs to tell customers, both internal and external, about the change.

You cannot hide away and hope they forget you told them the new platform was coming next month when, in actual fact, it will not be delivered until next year. This is basic stuff, but it is rarely executed consistently. Being honest with customers is the foundation to building strong relationships. Customers understand that projects run over. They understand that the software can't do everything, and they understand that development takes time. However, customers get grumpy when their expectations are not met. Maintaining strong relationships with customers requires setting appropriate and realistic expectations (which includes saying no sometimes) and updating those expectations regularly as circumstances change.

Defined processes and ownership, consistently enforced, reduce the amount of unrealistic expectations hiding in the customer base. Setting clear objectives, assigning ownership, and requiring accountability can be the difference between a smooth transition to a new platform and a bumpy one. Chunky corporates can get closer to their customers via one extremely important advantage they have over lean startups. Yes, you read that right – there is an advantage to being a chunky corporate: a long history of usage statistics. What chunky corporates have that lean startups do not is a legacy platform. That platform provides valuable insight into how customers interact with the system. Understanding what customers like and don't like about the old platform is critical to making sure they appreciate the new platform.

# Don't Forget to Sunset the Old Products

When undertaking a replatforming exercise, appreciate that asking a customer to change is a big request. People don't like change, and customers want an easy life. This is especially true of customers giving up some features. Product and technology teams need help from their customer-facing colleagues to manage the customer base. If they are worried about whether or not the new platform will be as good as the old one, or if they fear that it will take a significant amount of time for them to adjust to the new platform, they will rebel against a planned migration. This can stifle your ability to sunset the old products.

Product is responsible for determining which features or product will be sunset. Usage statistics, relationships with users, and a deep understanding of the competitive landscape are the keys to successfully identifying which features to sunset. Once that is decided, it should be proactively communicated to customer-facing teams and to technology. After it is communicated, features should be deprecated and phased out over an agreed timeline. Ideally, features identified for decommissioning should be deprecated in the legacy platform well in advance of a planned migration to a new platform in which those features will not exist.

# Five Critical Elements to Replatforming the Right Way

1.  Define the vision.

2.  Get the data right first.

3.  Design, execute, and check.

4.  Get close to your colleagues and customers.

5.  Don't forget to sunset old products.

These provide a useful framework for managing a replatforming project. Within this framework, though, we must also consider if the method for execution is appropriate. As we have shown, Lean-Agile is regularly misapplied to replatforming projects. It is incompatible with the defined set of milestones laid down by the legacy platforms a chunky corporate has built or acquired previously. To replatform successfully, we need to adapt Lean-Agile in the face of chunky corporate constraints.

# Replatforming Execution

In this section, we will look at best practices for executing a replatforming exercise. Lean-Agile principles are widely accepted as best practice in software development. DevOps and Scaled Agile (SAFe) methodologies adapt these principles for operational application in large organizations. As such, business leaders assume Lean-Agile is the best way to run *any* software build. The application of these methodologies to a replatforming exercise, however, is misplaced.

The business outcome sought via replatforming is the substitution of outdated software with a more productive software system that enables users to achieve defined goals. In laypersons terms, replatforming enables users do to the same thing they did before, just better and faster. This is diametrically opposed to the methods proposed by Lean-Agile principles. Lean principles dictate that the product roadmap be dynamic and innovation-focused. Agile promotes responding to change over following a plan. Lean-Agile asks that we move the goalposts regularly based on market feedback.

When you are replatforming, however, your product roadmap is defined. You do not have the freedom to move goalposts. You are answering to a larger set of stakeholders: investors, customers, colleagues – whose expectations constrain your movement. Replatforming starts with the list of features that already exist on the legacy platform(s) and cannot be sunset. Those are the goalposts. That is the MVP. Your MVP, when it was created originally, took years to build and refine. Back in Chapter 2 we reminded readers that Eric Ries never intended Lean Principles to be applied to a rebuild, which requires focused execution to enable predictability. There is nothing inherently wrong with Lean-Agile; it is just not the right methodology for replatforming. Table 7-1 explains the differences.

***Table 7-1.*** *Lean-Agile is not the right methodology for a software replatforming project because successful replatforming is stable, predictable, and relies on focused execution*

|  | **New Build** | **Replatforming** |
|---|---|---|
| Customers | No expectations<br>Want new features | Big expectations<br>Want stability |
| Product | Exciting | Boring |
| Board | Risky | Predictable |

Most chunky corporate replatforming projects are AINO (Agile in Name Only). The words *Lean* and *Agile* will pop up all over project plans and presentations to the board. They will be sprinkled throughout customer conversations regarding the release of new product features. But in the back corridors, whispered under breath, colleagues are shaking their heads with incredulity.

Amari: "The Board mandating that we define the roadmap and timeline for the entire project means we can't really follow Lean-Agile principles."

Caroline: "Don't the people running this place know that you can't have an Agile project when the features, timeline, and budget are pre-defined?"

Amari: "What about Scaled Agile? That SAFe methodology for large projects?"

Caroline: "SAFe, like Lean, is focused on innovation. Our leadership team doesn't want product innovation. Innovation is too risky. They want us to deliver the project on budget and in the agreed timeline. We are going to be laser-focused on execution of defined features to hit the timelines they want us to hit."

Amari: "I guess we'll just keep calling it Agile and hope they don't notice that we are actually running a Waterfall project because our MVP has to be a fully-fledged platform that does everything the previous platform did and more before any of our customers will consider using it."

Caroline: "Look, what we present to the leadership team and what we do behind the scenes are not going to be the same thing. We just have to find a way to deliver."

This single nugget of divergence can be a seed that sprouts conflict across a project. It starts innocently enough with developers and product owners whispering under their breath that the leadership team is in la-la land if they think an inflexible roadmap with discrete timelines is Lean-Agile. When things start to get off track, though, there is a fissure between the leadership team and the engineers that is then ripe for exploitation. A deadline is missed. Technology managers come under pressure to get the project back on track, and that pressure flows downhill.

Now the conversation changes from a genial, "Our leadership team is in la-la land," to a more negative, "What they are asking of us is impossible." With that, the door has opened to *us* and *them* mentality. Before you know it, the engineering team feels like an insular group that is misunderstood and persecuted. They stop communicating with other teams because they feel disgruntled. Senior leadership and other teams become *them*, and the engineers start to retreat into *us*. This retreat makes it very difficult to foster collaborative, communicative environments and makes it incredibly difficult to deliver efficiently. By retreating from colleagues, engineering teams exacerbate the issue. Feature delivery starts to diverge from desired outcomes.

Chunky corporates do not have the luxury of executing Lean-Agile products, because the endgame is defined and the timeline is fixed to an investment cycle. The goalposts are in sight; they are not some misty magic treasure to be uncovered. The team is working toward a defined set of features grouped into key initiatives, milestones, features, and epics. In a chunky corporate replatforming exercise, success means efficiently building a long list of defined features. If you are building a house, your first goalpost is the living room. As soon as it is released, you are on to the next goalpost: the kitchen. On your predefined list are the elements that will make a brilliant house: four bedrooms, two and a half baths, a garage. No one will move into the house until the rooms are built and the place is habitable. A chunky corporate has to reach all of the goalposts, before its customers will move in. *Moving in* in this scenario means stopping using the old platform and starting to use the new platform.

Why is this diametrically opposed to Lean-Agile methodology? The ability to step back and research before deciding to pivot or persevere is a fundamental element of the combined principles of Lean-Agile methodologies. If you are building a house and the customers already moved in, you don't have the luxury of stepping back after the living room is built to see if you should move on to the kitchen next. Your family has expectations the kitchen is coming next. By the time you pivot, the family have already cancelled their subscription to your building service and moved out. They didn't move out because the living room was terrible. They moved out because the development roadmap didn't reflect their preconceived notions of what a house should be. It's the same when you are replatforming.

If we were to be truly Lean-Agile, when the Joneses move into a living room and decide they need to move the electric outlets and window so they can put a TV on the south wall, we move the electrical outlets and the window for them before moving on to build the kitchen. We might even build two living rooms: one with electric outlets and the window on the south wall, and one with them on the west wall, so the Joneses can see which configuration works better. (This is the housebuilding equivalent of split testing.)

We might put a fake door in the living room with a sign that reads, "Kitchen," to see if the Joneses want a kitchen. If family members regularly push on the door, we can feel confident they want a kitchen. Can you see how these methods are much more powerful if you don't have a preconceived notion of what a house looks like? We know that a kitchen is more important to the Joneses than whether or not the electric outlet is on the south wall or the west wall. We don't need a fake door to tell us that. All we are doing is pissing off the Joneses by making them think there is a kitchen, which they expect, when there is just a fake door. It is not in the interest of a leadership team to spend resources moving outlets around in the living room when there is a kitchen to be built.

This conundrum does not mean, however, that we should revert to Waterfall principles. Lean-Agile development methods have gained popularity for a reason. They are very good at driving efficient, collaborative development. That being said, we need to stop hiding the fact that replatforming exercises are not really Lean-Agile and that we need to find a new way to describe them. It is important to empower engineers to deviate from Lean-Agile methods and adopt what I call a Goal Orienteering approach to replatforming software development.

# Goal Orienteering

Orienteering is a sport in which teams navigate to defined waypoints on a map as fast as possible. Defined goals, in software development, are at odds with Lean-Agile principles. Replatforming software is more like Orienteering and less like Lean-Agile. You are given a set of waypoints (your milestones). How you reach them is up to you, but the waypoints are fixed. You do not have the freedom to explore new product development in multiple directions when you are rebuilding an existing product stack.

Remember the example when Caroline and her team had lost their point of orientation trying to manage a complex sprint plan? They went snow-blind because they lost sight of the goals in all the noise generated by a complex, interdependent sprint plan. Orienteering strives to provide a set of common goals to provide consistency and context to the sprint plan. With an Orienteering approach, we provide new boundaries within which engineers work to adapt Lean and Agile principles in the face of constraints imposed upon us by replatforming. This enables the broader team of cross-functional stakeholders to reach greater alignment and work more efficiently as a result.

Katie: "Blake, John, can I be honest with you?"

Blake: "I hate when she says that."

Katie: "You have to stop using the terms 'Lean' and 'Agile.'"

Blake: "What? I thought Lean-Agile was the best way to build software."

John (*shaking his head*): "I know. They are terms we throw around like we are applying them appropriately, but everyone down in the weeds knows we're neither Lean nor Agile. I see the eye rolls every time I say we have to get leaner or be more agile."

Katie: "So give them something better. Get them Orienteering."

John: "Isn't it just syntax? I mean, we are still talking about two-week sprints and regular releases, right?"

Katie: "Yes, we are still talking about two-week sprints and regular releases. Teams will still work in Scrum or Kanban. But, much more importantly, we work toward agreed waypoints throughout the project that are defined. It is not a huge shift to move from Lean-Agile to Orienteering, but it is an important one. Lean-Agile principles are designed around rapid innovation. What you will build is based on market feedback in these methodologies. Don and the Board don't want innovation. They want to be clear on what gets built next. They want predictable delivery of defined milestones."

The goals are in fixed positions. We know the milestones we have to deliver. How we design, document, and deliver them is where we have flexibility to innovate. We want the high-collaboration approach to software development espoused in Agile. However, in a replatforming exercise, we cannot sacrifice documentation in favor of working software as Agile may espouse. Orienteering relies on meticulous documentation of scope, architectural design, and requirements because it requires alignment across a large number of stakeholders over a long period of time.

We want to release early and often and continuously improve our applications. An Orienteering approach to replatforming retains these elements of Lean-Agile methodologies. However, we get rid of the expectation that the product roadmap is fluid and that our primary objective is to develop new products for undefined markets. We accept that replatforming bears some unavoidable similarities to Waterfall. Table 7-2 summarizes these differences.

***Table 7-2.*** *The Orienteering approach takes the best of Lean-Agile principles and adapts it to the constraints of replatforming*

|  | Waterfall | Lean-Agile | Orienteering |
|---|---|---|---|
| Feature definition | Fixed and detailed | Vague and flexible | Fixed and detailed |
| Timeline | Fixed | Flexible | Fixed |
| Team structure | Hierarchical | Scrums | Scrums and squads |
| Cross-team collaboration | Limited | High | High |
| Roadmap | Defined and fixed | Flexible | Defined and flexible |
| Release schedule | At completion | Continuous integration/continuous deployment | Continuous integration/continuous deployment |
| Pace | Cadenced/regular | Rapid/extreme | Cadenced/regular |

In a goal-based Orienteering project, flexibility and innovation are focused on how we rebuild existing features, not what the features will do. The *what* is defined: we need a kitchen. Where we want to focus innovation is on *how* we solve those problems. How could the kitchen be reimagined to work better? How could it be designed and built more efficiently, knowing all that we learned from building and using it the first time? Rather than spending our innovation resources on determining if the Joneses want a kitchen, we spend it on understanding if they want an open plan style or galley. [Here's a hint: they want open plan; no one wants a galley kitchen.]

In an Orienteering approach to replatforming, how you make our way from architectural assets to a web application (or set of web applications) that deliver those features is open and flexible. We start with the set of features, grouped into milestones, that are already in use across your customer base in your legacy platform(s): a living room, a kitchen, three bedrooms, and two and a half baths. Remove any features from this list that are no longer used or can be successfully sunset without putting our customer base at risk. The Joneses no longer use the garage for cars, so when we build the garage, we will convert the space into storage for bikes and garden tools, plus a mud room. This is how you define the *what* for each feature.

You develop an understanding of what the feature does, and why the customer uses it. The key is to stop short of defining how these features will be coded. We want to retain flexibility in the design approach and execution. We don't want to predefine the *how* or bias our teams by assuming that all the features will be built as they were before. Some features may not be built natively, for example, instead they may leverage third-party tools.

Chunky corporates should see this as an advantage over a lean startup. A lean startup, in contrast, will spend a great deal of energy identifying the *right* features to build. A chunky corporate already knows the right features to build and has a mature customer base using them. The least efficient outcome would be for Acme to spend lots of resources identifying the *right* features to build when it knows its existing customers will use the ones it has!

Unless they really muck up the quality of the new features, Acme should see similar if not improved usage on the new platform after customers are migrated. Chunky corporates do not need to build a customer base from scratch. They need to keep the existing customer base happy while continuing to grow. The chunky corporates of the world should embrace this fantastic advantage and build upon it, rather than trying to pursue Lean-Agile principles to a fault.

The other element of Agile usefully kept in Orienteering is regular release and iteration. How this element differs under Orienteering methodology as opposed to Lean-Agile, though, is in access to the production platform. Most lean startups build a production platform, or set of applications, upon which all features are available. In Orienteering, teams release code to a production environment, but hold back operational access to customers until the platform has reached parity with the legacy offering. A chunky corporate will likely have multiple production platforms. Each legacy platform will have a production environment, and the new platform or applications will, too. Testing of the new platform can be controlled via operational user access. Internal users can test the new production platform, or any new applications, in the same way they test legacy platforms. External users can be given access to the new platform to have a play around before they adopt it operationally.

In this scenario, customers maintain access to the legacy platform for daily use until the new platform is ready. This can be achieved through thoughtful governance of user access. With a defined product management configuration that governs what individual users see, half-finished features can be released to the production environment but hidden from customer view until ready. New applications can replace old portions of the legacy platform as they are completed if appropriate user authorization and authentication infrastructure is in place.

Throughout its replatforming projects, Acme can use colleagues and friendly customers to test the new applications and provide feedback on the quality of the new features. That feedback is incorporated into the project build but under the constraint that it does not impact the milestones. The critical point here is that feedback helps to identify design gaps or edge cases not identified in the build process. When feedback calls for a new feature that sits outside of the agreed milestones, it is not picked up directly by technology, but fed into the product team for more research and evaluation. It may be pursued in future, when all agreed milestones are delivered, but it would not be considered for immediate development, as that would impact delivery of pre-agreed milestones.

The aim of deploying this Orienteering method is to apply one of the core principles of the Lean Startup – the Build-Measure-Learn[1] feedback loop – but under the context of a defined product roadmap, rather than a vague one. You can still Build-Measure-Learn when working on an Orienteering-based project. The critical thing here is understanding that you will need some friendly customers (both internal and external) that are willing to devote time to testing the new platform before using it operationally. They won't be able to use a new platform operationally until they can accomplish the same tasks in it that they carry out in the legacy platform.

So, while continuous integration and continuous delivery/deployment remain in practice for Orienteering, customers probably won't use the deployed features fully. The environment to which features are deployed will probably only be used for testing until the point that users are willing to "flip the switch" from old platform to new. Wherever possible, teams should replace portions of monolithic legacy platforms with new, smaller, more contained applications, but the realities of legacy architecture or real world ways of working may make this nearly impossible.

---

[1] Ries, Eric. *The Lean Startup: How Constant Innovation Creates Radically Successful Businesses*. Penguin Random House UK, 2011.

The goals in an Orienteering project are usually pretty big: a complex subscription and billing application; a product application; a data migration. Each one could be the equivalent of a typical lean MVP. Once these are agreed, they remain relatively constant. There might be a few features that are added to the list if competitive dynamics shift quickly, or a few that drop off the list through customer attrition or negotiation.

In the grand scheme of things, though, the bulk of these large requirements must be delivered to facilitate decommissioning or updating of the legacy platforms that are no longer fit for purpose. These are the goals. They are documented in a common, accessible space so that all team members can understand the context and scale of what needs to be delivered. Pauses should be built into the sprint plan following the delivery of each goal. Highly pressurized replatforming exercises that go on for years cause people to burn out. Without appropriate pauses built into the timeline, team members will start making poor decisions, slowing the project down in the long run. Resources should be dedicated to this, and it should be factored into the project plan from the outset. Orienteering adheres to continuous integration and continuous deployment (CI/CD) methods for delivering small features that form part of larger milestones.

Teams must agree on the metrics that enable them to move on from one goal to the next. The baseline, as with Agile, is working software. However, Orienteering projects need to go further. Defined business outcomes should be associated with each goal: target percentage of payments made online; movement of existing customers from one application to another; target percentage of existing data accurately reflected in a new application. There is a balance to strike between scope creep and signing off features because they meet the definition of done. When a goal is reached, there is a pause built into the sprint plan to allow for cleanup and maintenance, but most importantly, to give the squads a break. The squads working to deliver them will need well-timed breaks to make sure the rest of the organization's software and infrastructure don't fall apart and don't end up in a huge hole of technical debt while the team is replatforming.

In Orienteering, how the team move from point A to point B is flexible, but arriving at point B as a goal is not. The goals are the touchstones that guide the project. The team can come back to them again and again; they are the natural pause points along a journey from old platform to new. At each of these waypoints, John and Blake should check in to ensure that the project is delivering on the business outcomes associated with the goals. These are reached only when agreed business metrics demonstrate success, not when a feature is signed off in DevOps. It is imperative that John and Blake keep Acme's software development teams focused on reaching these defined waypoints. They are the goals to which you navigate with a strong compass and an aligned cross-functional team.

# Key Takeaways

- Lean-Agile doesn't work well for replatforming exercises because it was conceived to enable constant feature innovation.

- Orienteering is a software development methodology that adapts Lean-Agile to work within the constraints a chunky corporate faces.

- Orienteering relies on focused discipline to deliver defined product milestones.

# CHAPTER 8

# Dealing with Data

Data. What a funny little magical word. I once spent an afternoon debating with an incredibly intelligent colleague whether we should continue to insist the word data is always plural or accept the evolution of grammar that allows writers to choose if the word is plural or singular. In case you are wondering, my position at the time was that datum is the singular; therefore, data should always be plural. His counterargument was that data can be treated in the same way team is treated as singular. It can be singular even though it represents a plural number of individuals. I'll leave you readers to draw your own conclusions on that point. My point here is that data people are big nerds who are critical to the success of a mature software organization and should be empowered to spend (some) afternoons debating ridiculous elements of data because it does their little nerdy hearts good.

For the early part of my corporate career, I worked for data companies whose main source of subscription revenue came from the information they provided to customers. Essentially, I was working for publication houses, but the publications weren't qualitative prose, they were books with hundreds of pages of tables containing economic data. When I first started out, we were still publishing actual books every quarter. These were mailed to customers alongside digital versions of tables that could be downloaded from our website. (My kids refer to this point in history, when Mom was young, as "the olden days.")

K. Tamblin, *The Lean-Agile Dilemma*, https://doi.org/10.1007/979-8-8688-0321-5_8

When we built our first web platform, we were given a very specific set of engineering resources and a fixed amount of time to create a web platform where customers could find and manipulate our data. I didn't realize it at the time, but because we were a data company, all of our decisions as a result were data-forward. We approached problems by looking at how data could solve them. We only resorted to bothering the engineering team if we couldn't find a data-based solution. We were economists, after all, not software engineers. As a result, our technology was not particularly innovative. It did the job, but we weren't lighting the world on fire.

Years later, I moved on and went to work for a software company. What I found in that transition astounded me. Colleagues at the software company always looked to technology to solve problems and dealt with data as a by-product of software workflows. As a result, the data collected and returned to customers by our technology were disorganized, fragmented, and extremely difficult to extract and analyze. I scratched my head a lot in those first few months of trying to come to grips with what was different at the two organizations. In the end, neither approach is correct; they both have shortcomings. What is comical to me, though, is the blindness with which different teams apply them. It isn't deliberate; people naturally look to what they know to solve a problem. Analysts who do not code won't look for solutions in software code. Software engineers, on the other hand, tend to look for coding-based solutions first.

So, what does it all mean and why should we care? Well, data and technology are intrinsically linked. If we can only see one side of that coin, we are doomed to inefficiency. The trick to striking the right balance is to get data-oriented and technology-oriented colleagues working closely alongside each other, to reduce the problem-solving bias. We should be aiming to apply appropriate, efficient solutions regardless of whether they adjust the data or the code. There are lots of job roles in this space: software engineers, database engineers, information architects, data scientists, and analysts are some of the most common.

Software engineers can tell you how the code can solve your problems. Database engineers can tell you how to store, push, and pull data. Information architects can document process flows and outline where the data will need to be available for the system to use. Data scientists can manage transformation processes associated with moving data between and across databases. Analysts have a valuable ability to look at data and find the story. Analysts can tell you why you should care about what the data say. They are the most likely to find errors. Engineers, architects, data scientists, and analysts should not work in silos. Analysts and data scientists should not operate in a separate bubble of activity. All of these experts have a role in the squad. This entire cast of characters should be involved in the design phase of any build, particularly when features are focused on data generation, data storage, and data organization. Only with input from multiple roles can a team rely on data to deliver its expected value.

The database engineer builds the foundation – providing the location and structure in which data will be stored. This could also be carried out by a database architect. Depending on the size of the organization, this could be one role or two. The software engineer builds the user experience around that foundation. The information architect outlines the workflows that users will follow and informs the structure of the underlying data required to deliver them. The data scientist moves data from source to target, providing meaningful transformations of data and ensuring data are accurate. The analyst translates data into meaningful insights for users and ensures the data are credible. These roles are explained in Table 8-1.

***Table 8-1.*** *Many roles and areas of expertise contribute to successful management of data in a technology ecosystem*

|  | Potential Strengths | Potential Weaknesses |
|---|---|---|
| Database engineer | Creates data infrastructure, data model, and practical data design | Lacks insight to how internal and external customers use data |
| Software engineer | Codes software, usually with a specialty in user interface, mid-layer or back-end | Overlooks how data structure can maximize value for end users |
| Information architect | Identifies which individual data points need to be available at various places in the platform | Documents data points in processes, rather than optimizing processes via data |
| Data scientist | Understands data transformations and manipulations, codes in Python or similar | Coding is limited to data languages, overlooks the story or credibility of data |
| Analyst | Unlocks the story data tell, great QA testers as they look at the content in an application, not just whether or not the application works | Often has little-to-no coding skills |

In a replatforming exercise, it is quite common to move a large amount of data from source data sets (A, B, C, and D) to a target data set "T." Most chunky corporates have multiple data sets across multiple platforms. If growth is acquisition-based, source data sets will be an inevitable consequence of bringing together varying product lines from legacy companies. For example, Company A is the origin company, with data set A. Company A acquires Company B with data set B. Company A acquires Company C with data set C, and so on.

The other common scenario is organic growth with decentralized controls. So, for example, Company A sets itself up and experiences significant growth. It sets up subsidiary B in a new region or industry, which requires slightly different data. So, database B is set up alongside database A to cope with the differences. So it continues. In either scenario, data sets A, B, C, and D have different data models and different methods for storing data. They respect different units, and it will be harder than you think to put the data sets together. Don't even get me started on aligning dates across the United States and the UK. Honestly, the amount of hours I have personally spent trying to reformat dates that go DD-MM-YYYY with dates that go MM-DD-YYYY makes me want to seriously reevaluate my self-worth. But here we are. Oh, and if you are wondering, the best way to name files with dates in the title is YYYYMMDD_Name. That way, they sort themselves in chronological order.

Acme, as a result of acquisitions and regional expansions has multiple origin data sets: A, B, C, and D. Blake has concluded, logically, that the resources required to maintain A, B, C, and D are not efficient, and Acme's Publishing Division should have a single platform that can access data from all of those sources, so its customers benefit from the breadth of global data. In laypersons terms, if data set A is North America and data set B is Europe, there may have been a time in which Acme's customers would have accepted having to access North American and European data on different platforms. They do not anymore. Acme's end customers do not want to spend hours aligning US date formats to UK date formats. They expect Acme to do that for them. So, now Blake, and the divisional CEO of Publishing, Tilen, find themselves replatforming, and one of the requirements of the new platform is that it can access all data sets A, B, C, and D seamlessly. As they bring together these data sets, overlapping data points must be aligned. There will need to be a universal anchor for data points that vary over regions, like date formats and time zones.

John is preparing George's development teams to start coding the new platform. The technology team is planning to replatform around data set A, and then move data sets B, C, and D into the data warehouse later. As soon as I see this in the program plan, I call Blake directly:

Katie: "Blake, have you noticed that the first phase of the plan ignores data alignment in favor of coding around data set A?"

Blake (*drawing his words out as if he is thinking while speaking and unsure what ambush awaits in my next sentence*): "Um, yeeeessss, I haaaave. Is that a problem in your mind?"

Katie: "Bad idea. Let me be more clear. This is a huge mistake, the fallout of which can take years to clean up. It's a huge red flag when a tech team thinks it can make data from different sources fit in an existing platform without testing the data first. Big mistake. HUGE. Let's get John on the phone and talk through alternative ways to organize the program."

Blake: "Ok. Stop scaring me. Let's get on it."

It is very rare that data can easily been manipulated to fit in an existing platform. Why? Because engineers cannot foresee all the little decisions they make every day that customize the code to the data in the database. If they do not have data from data set B on hand for testing at the time code is written, they will not see the issues that data variations will throw up in the code. If you think that your engineers can manage that, you are expecting the impossible of them.

I walk Blake and John through an example: I worked on a project in which the product platform asked customer companies to enter their company registration numbers. The MVP platform was built on UK data. Therefore, the in-line validation (the bit of code that prevents you from moving on if your data doesn't fit a pattern – like ____@____.com for an email address) was built to accept UK company registration numbers with a set of conditions. One of those conditions was that the registration number has to be unique. Another was that it only supports numeric characters. We then prepared to migrate our customers in Ireland and quickly discovered that registration numbers in Ireland are not unique to one company. We were being Lean-Agile and responding to changes as needed. However, we wouldn't have needed to change if we had all our global data in a single database when the code was first written. We thought it would be simple to keep adjusting the in-line validation with each new variation we found. Unfortunately, it wasn't that simple.

Updating the platform to support additional countries went beyond changing the in-line validation of registration numbers in the user interface (UI). We were forced to make underlying changes to the data model, which then had ramifications for code across the platform. See, when the data model was first built, it was assumed that company registration would be a unique number, like it is in the UK. When the CRM system configuration team went looking for a unique identifier for each company in the CRM, they chose company registration number. So, the CRM system was configured to align company records around their unique identifier: company registration number.

System notifications were managed in overnight batch processes, which used the company registration number as the identifier against which relevant notifications were stored. Once Irish data were incorporated, CRM workflows and notifications broke because company registration was no longer a unique company identifier. The team had to create a new, globally unique data field, called COMPANYID, that was different from the company registration number. Then, every workflow across CRM and the platform that was linked to company registration number had to be rewritten to use the COMPANYID data field. Have you lost your will to live yet?

How could this be avoided? Well, the global data had been in the database before the engineering team had started coding; company registration would never have been chosen as the unique company identifier. The team would have identified early that was an unsuitable choice due to duplications in the Irish data. The short version takeaway from this painful anecdote is get your data house in order first. It is very likely you will find that none of your existing data sets, A, B, C, or D, are capable of handling all data variations. Instead, you are going to have to build a new data set, T, with a data model that can support all the data variations found across data sets A, B, C, and D. Once your data have been migrated from your source databases, A, B, C, and D to your target database, T, then you can start building a set of software applications that work with T. This will minimize rework associated with bringing in large data sets during the build phase.

The other caveat I emphasize to Blake and John is that moving data from A, B, C, and D to T will not be a light undertaking. Acme will need a mechanism that can repeatedly move the data from the source databases, transforming any units that do not match the target, to the target database (an Extract, Transform, and Load, or ETL, process). The reason I recommend this is that Acme needs to support existing customers' legacy platforms, which depend on databases A, B, C, and D, while they are building and testing the platform that runs off data set T. I warn Blake and John of the dangers of thinking they can build the new platform, then stick all the data in it, and *flip a switch* to move customers on to it. Flipping a switch from one data set to another is a dangerous proposition. The more measured and less risky approach is to build the target data set, T, with a mechanism that can quickly move data from the source data sets to the target data set repeatedly. This mitigates against the risk of large-scale data issues preventing customer migration at the last minute.

It also enables the engineers to build a platform around real data from all sources, and that data can be kept up to date while customers continue to interact with the source data sets on legacy platforms. In this scenario, flipping the switch means doing a final data pull from all source data sets prior to migrating customers from the legacy platform(s) to the new platform that runs off of data set T. The benefit of having repeatable tools in place to practice this data migration over and over again is that it gives the team time to work out data issues. It also pushes the team to address data incompatibility issues (like time zone and data format) early in the coding process, preventing future rework. It reduces the possibility of a Major Validation Problem related to data. Investing early in data alignment will make future customer migrations go faster.

# Laying a Good Data Foundation

Blake asks me to meet with George's team to talk about the replatforming project in Publishing Division. I give George a call and ask him to get a meeting together for us and the data leads on the project. George organizes a face-to-face meeting with me, Julian, and Mikko. Julian is the information architect assigned to the project, and Mikko is the technical architect. We sit down, and everyone in the room looks at me nervously. I haven't been advising Acme for that long, but they get the feeling you only get hauled into a meeting with me if there is a suspected problem. I am gaining a reputation for asking difficult questions and being a general pain in the ass.

Katie: "Right, so, this is a totally informal meeting. I just wanted to get everyone together and find out a bit more about the approach we are taking to the data elements of the project, the phasing, and any challenges that potentially I could help with."

George: "Great, thanks, Katie. I've asked Julian to walk you through the program plan."

Julian: "Yes, absolutely. Thanks, George. We are starting with the Well-being product features. We've spent months looking at the data we collect from customers as part of the process of connecting schools with well-being practitioners, anyone from a yoga teacher to a therapist who offer services outside the regular curriculum, to schools. Through a number of acquisitions, we now have five different web platforms that connect practitioners to schools in their areas. We've aligned the information we collect from practitioners across all of these, and we've designed a new data collection form. The new platform will work off of the aligned data structure enabling us to put all practitioners on a single platform, connecting them to many more schools where they can sell services. We want to maximize the network effect of having so many schools and practitioners on the same platform."

Katie: "That's great, thanks. How many practitioners and how many schools are there in total, across all legacy platforms?"

Julian: "1,240 schools and about 10,000 practitioners."

Katie: "Can you walk me through the customer experience of moving from individual data collection forms to the common one?"

Julian: "No problem. So, if the practitioner-user has completed his or her online profile and background check, that status will come across to the new platform. If the user is in progress, we will ask that user to complete the process on the legacy platform, and bring the user across once the profile and background check are complete."

Katie: "Yes, that sounds sensible. Is the new application running off a new database?"

Julian: "Yes, we looked at the existing databases, but none are sufficient to house the volume and structure needed to manage the entire data set. We'll be better off starting fresh."

Katie: "Got it. At what point in the project does the user's data get moved from the legacy database into the new database? You know, beyond status *approved*, practitioner-users build up a lot of supplementary information: courses offered, historic course ratings, their qualifications and certifications. How does the data they entered previously get populated in the new database?"

*Eyes start to shift from Julian to George...George to Julian...Mikko to Julian...Mikko to George. Everyone shifts uncomfortably in their chairs like they are confused.*

Katie (*after an uncomfortably long pause*): "Can you walk me through the data journey? So, like, I'm a practitioner, and I've entered all this data about myself so you can carry out a background check. I'm *approved* because I've passed my background checks and my profile is complete. I am migrated to the new system. I log in, go to my profile. What do I see?"

Julian: "Well, you would have to enter your profile data again, but your *approved* status will be there, so schools can still find you in a search. You'll have twelve months to update your profile."

Katie: "Ok, just to make sure I understand. Practitioner-users of the system will have to re-enter all of the data that they previously entered into the legacy platform?"

Julian: "Yes, but we'll give them a pdf version of their old profile...you know, to make it easy. See, the new profile has different data fields from the old one. Mapping that across would be a nightmare."

Katie: "Yes, I understand the data structure is changing. Do you think that wiping a user's profile, though, might have implications for customer churn? If I've been considering using a competitor's Well-being network for a while, but can't be bothered to switch because my profile data is already set up in Acme's platform, when I discover that I'm going to lose my profile data in the Acme platform, that might just be the prompt I need to move to a competitor."

Julian: "Well...I mean...maybe, but I wouldn't think that would have a large impact."

Katie: "I see. We should give this some thought. I'm not sure I agree, but I need to understand the risks better before forming a strong opinion."

*45 minutes later*

Katie: "Blake, Tilen, John, have you got time for a quick chat?"

Blake: "Yes, we'll grab a meeting room."

*In the meeting room...*

Katie: "Right, so I had a chat with Julian and George. Maybe I'm way off, but are the team agreed that user data will not be migrated from legacy platforms to the new platform? Are we ready to manage this with customers?"

Tilen: "Excuse me?"

John: "First I've heard of it."

Blake: "Um, I'm pretty sure we set expectations that absolutely customer data should be available in the new platform."

Katie: "Ok, that is what I would have expected. Maybe Julian, George, and I had a miscommunication, but I don't think they have factored into the plan any development time for data migration. From what I understand, only the status of *approved* or *not approved* will be populated in the new database."

John: "Shit."

Katie: "Like I said, let's find out before we freak out, but I think we need to look at the plan and get aligned around the expectations for the customer journey."

Fast forward four weeks, and the team is now working on a revised program plan that includes resources set aside for data migration. I reconvene previous players George, Julian, and Mikko. I ask them to walk me through the technical plan. I ask Mikko to show me the design associated with moving data from the legacy databases to the target database.

Mikko: "Sure thing. You can see these process flows demonstrate how the data will flow from legacy databases to the new database. We should only need to move the data once. We are developing an Extract, Transform, and Load (ETL) routine to execute the plan."

Katie: "Do you have the ETLs designed for all of the legacy databases?"

Mikko: "Hopefully they won't need too much adjustment from one database to the next. We'll be running this in parallel to scrums starting to code. So, they can get to work on the features while we get the data ready."

Katie: "I get that will enable you to start coding sooner, and, in theory, seems like the best way to get things done quickly. However, it carries a high risk that you will encounter data issues down the road. Will we be able to rerun the ETL process repeatedly until we get the data transformations right?"

Mikko: "The ETLs aren't really designed to run repeatedly, though, I guess technically we could adjust them so that they do."

Katie: "In my experience, the first time you run it, you will find a substantial amount of data gets stuck along the way. I worked on a project once in which a surprising amount of data got lost somewhere in the extract from the legacy system, the transformation, and the load to the new system. We were a few days away from going live with customers, and only five percent of the data successfully made to the target database. It was a disaster. It ended up delaying customer adoption by six months. Trust me; it is important that we get the data in the target database early in the process."

Mikko: "Yikes. Surely we can do better than five percent."

Katie: "I am sure you can, but let's not plan on it being perfect first time through. It worries me to hear you say that you only need to move the data once. I would rephrase that to say you only need to get the data right once. You might have to move it repeatedly in order to get it right."

Effective projects have the right experts delivering in the appropriate areas. And yet, many organizations will leave an entire replatforming exercise to the technology team. The assumption in that approach is that replatforming is a *technology* thing. Of course, it *is* a technology thing. But if you are a data-enabled business, it is also a *data* thing. We have to stop thinking of data as something that sits inside a platform and start thinking of data as the skeleton off of which our applications hang. Applications are the muscles that flex and connect, but data are the backbone.

The optimal approach to problem-solving is to have people with data skills working closely with people who have technology skills in order to get the right mix of data and technology focus in the solution. This is not natural for people working in hierarchical organizations, though. Mikko is comfortable working within George's technology team, but asking her to go make friends in Kat's Data Science team pushes her out of her comfort zone. Even if she agrees in theory, George is going to have to manage Mikko carefully to ensure she actually changes her behavior and works effectively with Kat on a collaborative approach to the problem. If this is not monitored closely, there is every chance Mikko will go to Kat and say, "Hey, Kat, Katie said your team should pick up the ETL process. Can you get started on that, and let me know when you have a plan pulled together?" If I were omnipotent and could see this happening, I would appear in the room at that very moment.

Katie: "Mikko, I am sorry you interpreted my comments to suggest that you should delegate the ETL process to Kat. That was not my intention. I am now going to lock this door from the outside and you two are not allowed out again until you have a *collaborative* plan on how to extract the data (probably tech-led), transform the data (probably data science-led), and load the data (probably tech-led). Underpinning the plan should be a jointly agreed target data structure that enables us to extract maximum value from the data we hold."

Now, admittedly locking colleagues in a room until they get a job done has fallen out of fashion and breaks a number of human rights laws, but the point is people in hierarchical organizations do not naturally step out of their tribal mindsets in order to collaborate effectively. However, if you give them time to build personal relationships and put the right incentives in place to enable them to be successful, it can make collaboration part of the business fabric. In fact, collaboration across expert stakeholders works much better than the traditional hierarchical approach.

## Flexible by Design

Configurable software works based on products to which a user subscribes, not the workflows he wants to execute. Rigid software is organized by user workflows. For example, this type of user can see this button, which takes her to another page, which presents a set of information. Configurable software has sets of pages, functions, and content. These elements are combined in the platform based on the product purchased. Instead of a different dashboard for every type of user, multiple users have access to a single dashboard, and the features, functions, and content visible to the user are governed by the purchased product. Building software in this way requires a data-first mindset.

Data-driven companies typically employ more analysts than developers (or did traditionally) and look for solutions in the data before deploying technology to solve problems. SaaS players typically employ more developers than analysts, and look for solutions in code, not content. Top performing companies have a good balance of analysts and developers who understand and deploy both data and tech solutions appropriately. The highest performing coders, analysts, and data scientists pair problem-solving skills with intellectual curiosity that prompts them to seek out the best solution to a problem, not the one that falls within his or her comfort zone. Analysts understand the natural limits of data and collaborate proactively with engineers to find intelligent and efficient solutions to problems. High-performing engineers understand where adjustments to the underlying data can address problems more effectively than writing code.

In mature organizations with large teams, these functions have been separated into specialist silos with very little incentive to collaborate cross-functionally. Analysts and data scientists get frustrated by what looks like slow progress of code development as they observe replatforming projects from the outside with very little knowledge of the deep complexity software requirements contain. Developers, equally, are segmented into information architecture (IA) roles, engineering roles, and technical architecture (TA) roles. While they may collaborate in the design phase of a particular feature or milestone, very rarely do these roles continue collaborating throughout the build phase.

Mikko and Julian, as specialist TA and IA resources, support multiple scrums. It is very easy for them to agree on a design for a particular feature and move on to the next one before the feature is written in code. However, that leaves a lot of in-build decision-making to more generalist engineers who may not have the full context of the design. Mikko and Julian must find a way to stay close to the delivery of their designs without being part of the scrum, which is tricky. By defining cross-functional squads that include the scrum plus experts relevant to each goal, we can encourage close alignment during delivery. In short, Mikko, Julian, and Kat may never be part of a scrum, but they should be consulted by the scrum throughout the project as key decisions arise. They are important members of the squad, responsible for supporting the scrum throughout the build.

It is incredibly important that IA resources collaborate proactively with data scientists and analysts in the crafting of the underlying data model of a new system. However, the collaboration should not end there. It is common for the IA team to sketch a data model but leave all existing data where it is. Meanwhile, engineers start coding a platform on the assumption that the data will fit in beautifully when it is built. There are some practical reasons that most companies approach replatforming exercises in this way. The primary reason is that it is a pain in the neck to build real-time (or even batch process) data flows that will keep data in an old platform commensurate and synced with the new platform. It seems inherently inefficient: why would I move the data into the new platform before the platform is built? Then I have to keep it up to date, or move it all again when the platform is done. That just seems silly.

However, it is not silly. In fact, what most companies underestimate is the complexity of the data they hold and the inconsistencies and exceptions lurking within it. Understanding the shape of the data and resolving data conflicts is critical to having an efficient operating platform. After my conversation with Mikko, I am talking through my concerns with Blake, Tilen, John, and George. I get the feeling that George, especially, thinks that he has it all figured out. He doesn't understand why he is being asked to collaborate with another team on data design. He has already thought of everything, he thinks. My experience tells me he is being arrogant, though, and it is going to come back and bite him.

I worked for a multi-billion dollar information and technology firm that acquired over forty companies over a ten-year period. Founded in the late 1950s, it started as an industry publication company, much like Acme's Publications Division. Over the years, it grew and acquired a number of brand names in industry data and journalism. Many of these businesses started as print publications. They had teams of product managers that had or were in the process of moving PDF publications and Access, SQL, or Excel databases online. The company undertook a project to bring online content together with print content in a common portal called Connect [Connect is a really popular name choice for replatforming projects – I've worked on three Connect projects, and I promise I didn't name them!]. Each product manager across the business had a remit to get the data and written content associated with his or her team loaded to the portal. Connect was a large multi-million dollar investment, with development teams dedicated to different aspects of the portal. Teams across the business were put in a queue, each one waiting its turn to be given development resources to either digitize content or migrate content from a legacy web platform to the new platform, Connect. Overall, it was a successful project.

However, what unfolded over the next five years holds valuable lessons for product managers everywhere. The leadership of the project, and of the company, made an assumption that the organizational structure of the business would be sufficient to ensure any cross-team synergies were built into the platform organically. The data structure was dictated in silos by the individual teams writing requirements for different parts of the web portal. Data in one part of the portal for macroeconomic forecasting customers, data elsewhere for industry planners, another section for supply chain data, and so on.

Here was a missed opportunity: there was no common data backbone underpinning the system. Data were fragmented, with areas of unnatural overlap. There was no shared search or selection process offering users access to all data sets. We had missed the opportunity to create a sum greater than its data parts. Cross-sell and value synergies were overlooked because the team saw the data as elements sitting within various applications, not the backbone of the technology system.

My experience makes me follow up relentlessly with Mikko. We work together to map out key stakeholders from product, technology, and the business to get the right data design. Before any coding starts, these stakeholders have achieved clear alignment around the data fields that will be available, the shape and structure of the data, and how infrastructure will carry that data to and from the databases in which they are stored to the user interface. They walk me through the output of their efforts.

Mikko: "Katie, you'll be glad to know we've finished the data design. We are all aligned on what the data will look like, how the ETL process will work, and how we can migrate customer data."

Katie: "Great! When will it be finished so we can start building the application?"

Mikko: "Oh, wait, no, sorry. We've finished the design. We have this spreadsheet that maps all the data into a common data structure. But we need to build the platform first, then we will put the data in it right before we go live with customers. We'll build the platform using dummy data."

Katie: "Wrong answer."

Mikko: "I'm sorry?"

Katie: "That is the wrong way around. You are going to move all data into a common database before you build the platform. Dummy data is the root of all replatforming evil. Trust me. It is better data first, then software."

Mikko: "But data is the easy part. Let's do the hard part – the coding of the application – first, then we'll just pop the data in."

Katie: "Data is *not* the easy part. Last time I heard someone say that, I kept my mouth shut. Do you want to know what happened?"

Mikko: "I get the feeling you are going to tell me."

Katie: "One day before a major rebrand launch, and two weeks before planned customer migration, the team realized the platform couldn't support real customer data. They used dummy data in UAT [user acceptance testing]. When users tried to input real data, they couldn't. The system and data model only allowed for one document per user. However, if the team had looked at the actual data in the legacy platform, they would have seen each user was associated with multiple documents. They should have put the legacy data, including documents, into a common database first, then built the platform. Do you want to know how long the customer go-live was delayed?"

Mikko: "I don't think I do."

Katie: "Seven months. Customer migration was delayed by *seven* months to get it sorted. Needless to say, the CEO and the Board were pretty put out by the last-minute change in the plan and the extra cost required to fix it. This is not negotiable. Put real data, all of the real data, in a common database first. Then code the application based on what is in the database. I'm serious – it is for your own good."

Mikko: "Message received."

The other handy by-product of using real data is that it makes testing the platform much easier. Coders find hilarious jokes in dummy data. They'll use the boss's name, their favorite anime characters, and anything else that comes to mind. I have to admit, it works. It makes me giggle every time I open a platform for testing and find names like Chris P. Bacon in a search result. I'm easy to please, what can I say? Giggles aside, though, there is a downside to these office hijinks. When we use dummy data, we train our QA testers to ignore silly things, like a customer named Mickey Mouse.

Too often QA testers see that the platform shows *something* in a field where there should be data but do not check that *something* makes any sense whatsoever. They become blind to the actual data. They assume either the practitioner actually has a name of "Mickey Mouse" or they assume they are looking at dummy data. Instead of letting a QA tester make those assumptions, add acceptance criteria that has real data, and ask your QA team to check specific practitioner profiles to ensure that the data in your new platform matches the profile data of the same customer in your old platform. Until you can confirm that, you are not ready for customer migration. Do not put a date on your customer migration until that test is complete. And, ideally, get business testers – friendly colleagues who spend a lot of time supporting customers – checking it, too. They are much more likely to catch stuff like that, as explained in Table 8-2.

***Table 8-2.*** *Best practice requires that we leverage a range of appropriate skills to get data right before building software applications*

|  | **Good Practice** | **Bad Practice** |
|---|---|---|
| Collaboration | Match skills to needs | Follow org hierarchy |
| Specialist involvement | Throughout the dev cycle | At the beginning and end |
| Existing data sets | Use real data in UAT | Use dummy data in UAT |

Building the common data set first ensures that the software house is built on solid foundations. It ensures that future iteration of the product is straightforward and efficient, and it reduces the risk of future rework to back-end systems. Dummy data are not good enough for a replatforming exercise. Acme's customers care about their data. When a practitioner or a school user logs into the system, the first thing they will notice is whether or not the data they are used to seeing are correct. Data are everywhere in the platform; therefore, people using and testing the platform need to check it is accurate everywhere.

# Configurable Products

Product leaders seem doomed to learn the hard way that building scalable software products requires configurability. In my experience, unless a product owner or product manager has been burned by product inflexibility in the past, she will not proactively consider this. You don't know what you don't know, right? Chunky corporate history, though, can be an advantage. If you've built a software platform once before, surely you know what *not* to do the next time around. Knowledge of the past enables you to focus on new mistakes instead of making old mistakes over again (as mistakes are inevitable). Acme can harness its institutional knowledge, gained through a long history, to improve how its technology leverages data. That is much easier to accomplish when the data already exist.

However, even the best scrums need guidance and context to write efficient code. A product catalogue is a very important data element. The more complex it grows, the more data management it requires. At a lean startup, there does not need to be a grand plan of how hundreds of products will knit together across a complex software system. A lean startup shouldn't have hundreds of products! If you are a chunky corporate, though, already in the business of selling hundreds of products, it is worth investing the time and effort required to impart on your development team a shared understanding of how those products are going to be packaged and sold. Alignment on this front should be reached before writing the first line of code. If left unmanaged, it will become unmanageable.

Let's look at an example: For many years before joining Acme Tech's Analytics Division, product owner Jill worked on data-enabled products. The software products she managed delivered different data sets to different customers. In that environment, the back end data were consistent, and data sets were organized into small bricks that were then managed by product tokens. In this context, a product token is an element the application uses to determine if a user has access to a data set. This is not to be confused with blockchain tokens, which are more narrow in definition. Using a product token does not require a ledger or chain.

Some product managers refer to the concept as a feature flag: a data element that determines whether a user can see a feature or not. I prefer product token, though, because feature flag is more likely to be interpreted as relating to software features only. Product tokens can manage visibility of both software features and data sets, referred to as product blocks. When Jill worked on data-enabled products, each brick of data constituted a product, and products were grouped into packages. Jill sold packages to customers via subscriptions. Customers had user permissions managed in the system that allowed them to do a lot or a little based on the data packages to which they subscribed. This gave Jill great flexibility in her product stack. She could build data products from any imaginable combination of packages and sell them to customers in ways that enabled her to maximize the yield of the data set.

Since then, Jill has come to work for Acme's Analytics Division, supporting the analytics software platform. The Analytics Division has a long history as a software company, building workflow-based tools. Jill jumps straight into her new role, advising product owners on how to enhance the Productiva product line. She assumes the development teams working on Analytics Division software have a shared understanding of the terminology she uses: products, packages, subscriptions, and user permissions are all terms that had a common definition in her previous role.

Jill assumes that they carry the same meaning with her new colleagues. This isn't a conscious assumption; it is something she takes for granted. However, to her new engineering colleagues, these are foreign concepts. Workflow-based software in the Analytics division has always been driven by customer type, of which there are only two: Type A and Type B. The engineers and product owners at Acme ignore words like packages and products in user stories because to them, those are just the things in CRM that salespeople can sell. When they build software, what a user sees in the interface is based on his customer type. That is how it has always been done at Acme.

Jill and her supporting scrum team, called Minerva, led by scrum master, Kamilla, are preparing to build a new product. Jill assumes the engineering team will build a back office configuration function enabling features and data to be grouped into products. However, the developers in team Minerva don't share that understanding. Kamilla doesn't realize that Jill expects the concepts of products and packages to have a functional role in the user interface. When Kamilla reads the words products and packages in Jill's requirements, she inadvertently reduces their value. She and Jill don't have a common understanding of their definition.

When members of team Minerva ask Kamilla how to interpret these words, she tells them the words aren't important for the purposes of writing functional code. The design team and engineers, with guidance from Kamilla, assume that products are just what you sell, which is handled elsewhere, in the CRM system. They do not interpret products as being associated with pieces of data that inform the user experience. In contrast, Jill expects a product subscription to determine what the user can see or do in the web platform. Kamilla does not realize that she has assumed away this possibility.

When team Minerva builds the new product page, the interface checks the customer type to determine what information is loaded onto the page. Jill expects the interface to check the product to which the user is subscribed, via an assigned product code, and load the information associated with that product. However, Kamilla assumed that every user of Customer Type A would have one experience in the platform, and every user of Customer Type B would have a different experience. Therefore, in her mind, the most efficient piece of data to check when loading a page is customer type, not product. When the design team and engineers started to build, their work was informed by their shared history of building tools based on customer type. So, while the concept of a product exists in the data model, it doesn't drive platform behavior in the way Jill expects it to. Instead, platform behavior is driven by customer type, and the product code is only referenced in the subscription and billing part of the portal. The design team expects that all future requirements can be served by aligning customer experience to customer type.

So, how does Jill eventually figure this out? Well, it isn't something that is obvious in early testing. The platform works; it meets the listed acceptance criteria. Customer Type A and Customer Type B are subscribed to different product codes, so when Jill logs in as different users, she sees different information on the page. What Jill can't see is behind the user interface. Many months later, when Jill wants to make the packages more sophisticated, she finds this more difficult than expected. Jill writes up requirements to enable a dual-role customer of type A+B who purchases a package with products from each customer type domain.

The new package is created in the CRM system. It is configured in the back-end of the software. Jill logs in to see her lovely, combined package in action. It doesn't work. Jill is unable to deliver on the revenue targets associated with the new Productiva package. It takes days of discussion for Jill and Kamilla to finally understand the root cause of this miscommunication. The new product page builds a user experience based on the wrong factor, simply because Jill and Kamilla made different assumptions about the meaning of the words: products, packages, and subscriptions. Both Jill and Kamilla's assumptions are direct results of their previous experiences.

If you ask yourself why Lean-Agile projects work best with small teams sitting next to each other, the answer is simple. They talk. They talk constantly. They naturally reduce the number of communication gaps at each handover point by being in regular contact with each other. They have more opportunities to realize that they have different assumptions because they regularly align around decision points. They are more likely to ask when coding, "Hey – should the page load run off package or customer type?" These sorts of questions fly from the mouth of the developer to the ear of the product owner live as the developer is coding. In my head, this team is in some hipster coffee shop inside a WeWork office in London, rocking top knots and contoured facial hair while munching avocado toast or having just been to the cereal bar in Shoreditch. They are equal parts glamour and unicorn: gorgeous to look at and nonexistent at chunky corporates.

In contrast, large corporate development teams aren't likely to be in the same country, let alone the same office. Jill is based in the United States. Kamilla's team is based in Eastern Europe, and they are making decisions about what data points drive the UI page load live as they are coding because Jill's user story isn't clear to them. It's 3 a.m. in Boston, so Jill isn't going to answer an email for several hours. Does Kamilla wait seven hours, or make a decision and crack on with it? Naturally, the latter. This is how the gremlin lands in your platform. And then, when other coders look at previous code in order to answer the same question on a different page, it is like throwing water on Mogwai. The gremlin multiplies, and, before you know it, you have gremlins throughout your platform. By the time Jill realizes that the new page does not check the user's product code before loading content, there is a whole lot of code built onto Kamilla's assumption. She approaches Kamilla to estimate the amount of time required to change this and enable her new A+B package. "Six to eight sprints," Kamilla says. "We basically have to go back and rebuild the foundation."

If we are working in a world in which Jill and Kamilla don't sit side-by-side and aren't in regular communication throughout the build, they need to work off of the same data design and strategy. Product code is a data element. Customer type is a data element. Where Kamilla went wrong was in choosing the wrong data element for the job. Product requirements do not usually specify this level of detail. The data element that determines what a page loads is fundamental; it should be consistent throughout the platform. Something that fundamental is part of the technical design of the web system. It should be openly discussed, debated, and agreed upon before any teams start coding.

To enable a truly flexible product stack, a product ➤ package ➤ subscription approach should be at the heart of the entire web system and all related applications. This provides a natural hierarchy in which features are grouped into products, which are then grouped into packages, both of which (products and packages) can be sold on subscription. This hierarchy is described in Feature 8-1. Each application or page loads the relevant content based on the products or packages to which a user is granted access through a subscription (or a transaction in a non–subscription-based business). [I use the term "subscription" relatively loosely. Not all platforms are sold on a subscription basis, but for the purposes of simplicity, we will treat them in this exercise as if they are. It is, after all, the preferential sales model of the day, especially for data-driven software platforms.]

Using product tokens to determine what a user can access in any application carries additional benefit in a migration from old product to new. When new and old systems share a common data backbone and are product-driven, new products and old can be permissioned to customers simultaneously, enabling users to try out a new application before giving up the old. Old applications can be ramped-down in a relatively risk-free way, customer by customer if needed, when the removal of a product from the users' subscription renders the legacy application invisible.

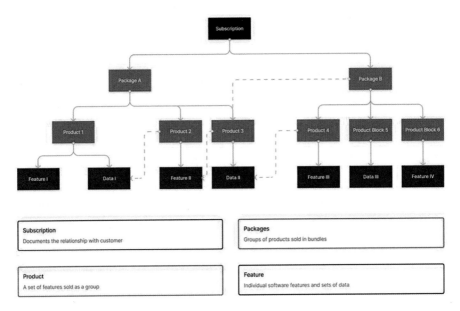

***Figure 8-1.***  *Product and package levels*

When design teams, or individual engineers, lacking in appropriate guidance, take a *persona-* or *organization-type* approach, they run the risk of effectively hard-coding the user experience based on preconceived and limited notions of what a user wants to do. The problem with designing a platform this way is that as soon as you think you've got it nailed, a new use case will crop up. A customer will come along and ask you to dismantle that workflow and add back more flexibility. Fixed workflow-based systems are notoriously inflexible. Data-driven systems, however, can be incredibly configurable.

When a system is designed around a user-product-package-subscription–based model, it can be configured to support many different workflows and many personas. A flexible system can cope with customers that purchase multiple products; let us not forget that selling more products to the existing customer base is a good thing. Software should easily cope with this. It is incumbent on product leaders to drive this efficiency throughout a replatforming exercise, especially if the previous platform was not built in such a flexible way. A key aim of any replatforming exercise is to deliver scalable, repeatable products that can be adjusted to meet additional customer requirements without requiring onerous rework. Any avoidance of rework we can reasonably achieve is worthwhile.

To be clear, the above approach assumes that platforms are multi-tenanted. By that, I mean software products in which multiple customers access the same applications. This sits in contrast with on-premise or single-tenanted platforms, which are naturally falling out of favor, except in specific circumstances. Multi-tenanted systems provide for a more scalable, repeatable, and typically more profitable product stack. Single-tenanted systems provide more data security, more options to customize, and come with a much higher price tag.

For most mid-size SaaS businesses, the approach of single-tenanted instances supporting a customized code base eventually becomes a burden the organization must carry. Over time, this sucks in maintenance resource like a black hole. Mid-size SaaS businesses should avoid this trap wherever possible by deep consideration of its target customers. Any feature that requires customization of the code to onboard a new customer should be heavily scrutinized.

# Key Takeaways

- Don't leave replatforming solely to the technology team. Appropriate solutions are cross-functional and leverage a data-first mindset.

- Dummy data should never be used to test a platform when real data exist.

- Data isn't a *thing inside the platforms*. Data is the backbone powering platforms.

- Product applications should be flexible and data-driven.

# CHAPTER 9

# Managing Customer Demands

Naturally, there is a relationship between a company's ability to deliver on the demands of its customers and its ability to grow revenue over time. However, there is often quite a large time lag between the two. Short-term revenue and profit performance are inefficient proxies for whether or not the product strategy is on track. These are flawed, wildly lagging indicators of the effectiveness of product strategy, especially in subscription businesses. If you operate in a business that sells annual subscriptions, each customer signs up for twelve months at a time and can typically only cancel once a year. This is a revenue model so attractive that every product on the planet seems to be chasing the elusive subscription model. You can even buy deodorant on subscription these days!

Subscriptions, though, can hide customer dissatisfaction. The longer the renewal cycle, the more divorced product effectiveness becomes from quarterly revenue measures. And yet, despite that being the exact thing that attracts investors to subscription models, it also quite often proves the Achilles heel of a chunky corporate. In subscription businesses, the key performance indicators (KPIs) that measure business performance are lagged substantially from customer satisfaction with the product. By the time you realize customers are seriously unhappy with your product, you are well behind the curve. And, if you are investor-owned, you won't have much time to turn your team's performance around once you discover customer dissatisfaction. Leaders at chunky corporates whose revenue

K. Tamblin, *The Lean-Agile Dilemma*, https://doi.org/10.1007/979-8-8688-0321-5_9

is flagging will quickly come under incredible time pressure to win back customers and compete in a changing marketplace. If they cannot, they will find themselves out of a job.

The examples of this same phenomenon in sport have become increasingly common. Coaches or managers having less than a year to turn team performance around have been attributed to sport being run *as a business*. For the purposes of illumination, we'll look at one of the most famous. In May 2013, just before the end of the UK Premier League football season, Sir Alex Ferguson announced his retirement as manager of Manchester United after twenty-six years of service. Ferguson's announcement came just a few months after long-time CEO David Gill announced he was stepping down after sixteen years with the club. The two most influential leaders at Manchester United were leaving. In May and June of 2013, three additional members of the coaching staff Mike Phelan, Eric Steele, and René Meulensteen departed the business. It was incredibly disruptive for the team and all colleagues at the business. David Moyes of Everton took over from Sir Alex, and in their first season with Moyes as manager, Manchester United endured some of its worst results since the 1980s. On April 22, 2014, with four games remaining in the season, Moyes was fired, less than one year into his six-year contract.

One could argue that the upheaval caused by the departure of a number of influential members from the club set Moyes up for failure. He had a virtually impossible task of maintaining team performance in the face of incredible change – a change the team had not experienced in a generation. Any manager would need time to build relationships with team members, understand the dynamic of the team, and set them on a new path under new leadership. However, when you have crowds of fans to answer to, and those fans are used to winning, time is not on your side (unless you are Ted Lasso).

Taken in this context, it reflects the reality that at most investor-owned businesses, poor short-term performance results in leaders getting fired. In this case, Moyes had less than a year to turn the team around. Business leaders face similar pressure when financial performance at a chunky corporate falters. Instead of answering to screaming fans, business leaders answer to screaming shareholders. Just like football fans, shareholders have a limited view of what is happening behind the scenes, and only a loose grasp on the nuances of what can improve productivity. In that context, they will demonstrate little patience for rebuilding a team. Instead, they will default to questioning business leadership as soon as financial performance stumbles and quickly call for leadership change when the business stops winning. But what if you actually have more time than you think to see poor financial performance coming? When you are running a subscription business, the signs will be there early, if you know where to look.

If a customer is disgruntled with a product on an annual subscription, it could take up to twelve months for that customer to cancel his or her subscription. In highly sticky products, it could take years for disgruntled customers to result in falling revenue. So, if renewal rates and bookings are the metrics by which you measure your business, you might be years behind the curve of customer satisfaction. Once the floodgates open to contracting revenue, it can take years to turn it back around.

Let's play out a typical timeline. Acme customer, Joanne, signs up for a three-year initial Software-as-a-Service (SaaS) subscription to Acme's Survey platform. Her subscription renews annually after the initial three-year period. Joanne renews her subscription, but over the course of year four, she starts to feel disgruntled. Requests for enhancements she asked for a year ago still haven't been delivered. Joanne wonders if Acme cares about her business. "Did my Acme account manager listen to my suggestions? Is there something better out there?" Joanne thinks about cancelling her subscription at the next renewal but needs six months to find an alternative solution and get sign-off on making the switch. Does Acme's leadership team see Joanne's frustration? And more importantly, if it is observed that Joanne is growing disgruntled, can Blake and the Acme team do anything about it?

The decision to act on Joanne's historic enhancement requests would have been made somewhere in the layers of product managers, product owners, developers, and application support specialists across the business: each with his or her own agenda, and each with a slightly different interpretation of the product strategy of the business. The people who hear Joanne's feedback will not be close to the people who can address it. If she is reporting something broken in the software product, that will be logged as a bug. But if she is requesting an additional feature, or making a suggestion for improvement, that will often get lost. For Joanne to see any action on her suggestions, she is dependent on proactive communication happening within the layers of Acme. The more layers between Joanne and the people who make product decisions, the less likely her feedback is to make it onto the product roadmap.

At a lean startup, Joanne can provide the same feedback, but it is much more likely to be handled in a way that keeps Joanne satisfied. Why? Because there are fewer layers between Joanne and the decision-makers. A lean startup doesn't have hundreds of account managers and customer service representatives. They are still *lean*. That means Joanne is likely to be treated like a human being, whose feedback is valued, and gets to the people who make the decisions. Lean startups need every customer they can get. So, if they don't agree with Joanne's feedback, or choose not to implement her suggestions, they are more likely to call up Joanne and let her know why. The leadership team of a lean startup is held to account by its customers. It hasn't got anyone else to satisfy. In contrast, a chunky corporate is beholden to multiple teams of leaders, from the operational senior leadership team to the Board and shareholders. The leadership team at a chunky corporate is managing layers upon layers of colleagues that sit between it and Joanne. And the leadership team is held to account by a Board, who doesn't know the individual employees by name, doesn't really know what they do on a day-to-day basis, and has never heard of Joanne or her feedback.

While, in theory, all of the appropriate incentives are in place for the organization to manage Joanne effectively, because there are many more handover points between colleagues, it is less likely to happen. Joanne is using Acme's web platform one day and decides she has a great idea for how it could be improved. She can't find her account manager's contact details, so she calls up Acme's customer service number listed on the website. A customer service representative, Gus, takes Joanne's call. There isn't anything Gus can do with Joanne's feedback; he doesn't make product improvement decisions.

Gus asks his boss, Smeeta, who he should tell about the feedback. Smeeta tells Gus to share it with the product team. Gus only knows one person in the product team, so he emails that person, Gareth, and shares the feedback. However, Gareth isn't in charge of the part of the product to which the feedback relates, so Gareth forwards the email to five different product owners across the team in one email asking that they get back to Gus. No one responds. They don't respond because the email was sent to five people. They all think someone else will respond. Are you losing track of the players and the feedback? Good. That's the point. It's like trying to keep track of the ball under the cup in a shell game.

Joanne's feedback gets lost. Now, imagine that over the course of a couple of years, this happens to Joanne on multiple occasions. Joanne thinks she is offering really good ideas for product enhancements. No one at Acme, though, seems to care. Certainly they aren't showing Joanne that they have any interest in implementing her suggestions. They aren't telling Joanne anything. She hears from her account manager, Janice, once a year at renewal time. Janice has never given Joanne an update on product enhancements and never asks follow-up questions about Joanne's feedback. If Gus hasn't proactively communicated Joanne's feedback to Janice, she may not even be aware of it. Gus communicating Joanne's feedback to Janice depends on him knowing, or being able to quickly determine, that Janice is Joanne's account manager.

At a lean startup, product development is responsive to customer demand. It is where the heart of the Lean-Agile software development method shines. Feedback loops are closed; developers are responsive; touch points between the customer and the development team are high. However, it is incredibly difficult to keep feedback loops closed as the number of relevant stakeholders rises. Agility requires coordination, and coordination gets harder the more people you have. Joanne's account manager, Janice, meanwhile, has no idea that Joanne is feeling disgruntled and ignored. Janice is shocked to get a cancellation notification after five years of managing what she thought was a pretty satisfied customer. If Janice was aware Joanne had provided many points of feedback over the last several years, most of which were not addressed, she could have seen it coming.

For chunky corporates to manage Joanne's feedback effectively, they need strong, clear lines of accountability. The first step is ensuring that an active decision is made regarding whether or not Acme will action Joanne's feedback. Then, that decision needs to be communicated back to Joanne. In the above example, though, players within Acme are playing hot potato with Joanne's feedback: each shrinking from what might be a difficult decision or conversation. Rather than disappoint a colleague or a customer, Acme's colleagues stay silent. Silence is the relationship killer. High-performing product teams must have clear expectations regarding customer feedback:

1. We do not ignore feedback from customers or colleagues; we make product decisions.

2. Decisions are communicated to relevant colleagues and customers proactively.

3. When decisions are complex, they are based on appropriate research.

4. When a decision is delayed due to competing priorities or lack of information, that delay is communicated to relevant stakeholders proactively.

Product owners want to do right by their customers but are overwhelmed by the amount of feedback coming to them. Many feel paralyzed by the pressure to make decisions that inevitably disappoint customers. Effective product managers are able to swiftly and proactively investigate whether or not action should be taken, make a decision, and communicate that decision, even to people that don't want to hear it. That requires analytical skills and people skills.

Unfortunately, most product managers (most people, actually) either tend toward the analytical or tend to be people-focused, which presents challenges that must be managed. A successful product manager can be either. Analytical product managers are great at using quantitative methods to make decisions and to manage a roadmap. People-focused product managers are great at getting the right people together to achieve a goal. The best excel in both areas, but these are mythical creatures, or, at a minimum, out of Acme's price range. In lieu of finding a mythical product manager, strong product leaders can build a team that has both analytical and people-focused members, utilizing their strengths where they are needed, rather than expecting everyone to be good at everything.

So, how do different product managers handle Joanne's feedback? An analytical product manager will analyze all sorts of usage statistics analysis to determine if Joanne's request for enhancement should make it on to the roadmap. This type of product manager will look at adjacent features' usage in the platform, build a model predicting usage of the new feature, model out the cost to deliver against the revenue it will drive in the organization, and prepare a ream of documentation explaining why it should or shouldn't be delivered based on numbers.

The people-focused product manager, on the other hand, may ring up multiple colleagues and customers, including Joanne, and gather all the opinions into a qualitative, consensus-driven thesis outlining whether the feature should be delivered. The best decision would take all inputs into consideration: usage of adjacent features, the competitive landscape, the business case, and the outcome Joanne is trying to achieve. So why doesn't this happen regularly? Well, most colleagues are not perfectly rounded in every way and do not (or cannot) gather all of the required research that would inform a fully rounded decision.

Ensuring that colleagues step out of their natural comfort zones to make informed decisions is one of the most important pillars of achieving sound product choices. Leveraging templates or pre-flight checklists ensure that a product manager has completed well-rounded analysis. This includes speaking to colleagues and customers about the feature, conducting usage analysis, and building a credible business case internally. The business case can be constructively challenged by peers within the organization, and it must include analysis of the opportunity cost. By choosing to spend resources on Joanne's enhancement, we are choosing to not spend resources on an alternative. What is the impact of that choice?

These steps provide the opportunity for Acme to align the layers that sit between Joanne and the product manager who makes the decision. The challenge is that people, when busy, will only do the bit they feel most comfortable with. So, typically, your people-focused product managers will spend ninety-eight percent of the information-gathering time talking to other people and canvasing opinions. The analytical product managers will spend ninety-eight percent of the information-gathering time staring at spreadsheets. Each will waffle and shuffle and divert attention when asked whether two percent was enough time to spend on the bit that was out of his or her comfort zone. Let's look at how this example plays out in Acme's Survey Division. Gareth asks Lily, "Hey, has anybody looked at that feedback from Joanne?" Lily realizes that it has fallen through the cracks, so she assigns it to team member, Dave.

Dave (an analytical product manager): "No, I haven't talked to Joanne. She's really busy."

Lily (Dave's manager): "Ok, what should we do? Should we wait for Joanne to be available? Have you tried talking to other customers like Joanne to see if they want the same feature?"

Dave: "No, haven't managed to do that yet. I will."

Dave (to Lily's manager, Lev): "Hey, Lev, I've done this great analysis to show that we should add this new feature."

Lev: "Fabulous. What does Lily say? Are we adding it?"

Dave: "Well, Lily wants to wait until Joanne comes back to us, but I don't think we should wait that long. I have a rock solid business case, and I say we go for it."

Lev: "Ok. I'll talk to Lily and see if we can get aligned."

There is nothing inherently wrong with the above as a single situation. What is quite common, though, is that it is not a single incident; it is indicative of a pattern. Dave is more comfortable in spreadsheets than in meetings with customers, so he leans on the analysis to make his case. He avoids meeting customers for feedback because it takes him out of his comfort zone. If Joanne had been free on the one day and time Dave tried to call her, he would have spoken to her. But because she didn't answer the phone and didn't call him back, he's quite happy to just leave her direct feedback out of the decision.

He creates pressure to move forward by going around Lily and speaking to Lev directly. Unless Lily and Lev are completely aligned, Dave will get his decision accepted with only half the relevant information. It takes strong and persistent leadership to insist product managers make good product decisions. It is down to human nature: if someone likes an activity (e.g., analyzing data, and, yes, some people actually like that activity), he is more likely to do that activity. If a person feels slightly out of his comfort zone calling customers, for example, he is less likely to carry out that activity, or more likely to give up if the customer doesn't answer on the first ring or respond to the first email. These tendencies, if left unaddressed, can lead to systemic bias in product decision-making.

Let's look at the alternative scenario in which Lily assigns this exercise to Dave's colleague, Kate. Kate prefers spending time with people to staring at spreadsheets. In Kate's workday, she's much quicker to jump on the phone with customers and speak to colleagues to make a decision. Imagine the same scenario as above, but it is Kate who owns the decision, not Dave. Kate (a people-focused product manager): "No, I haven't seen the usage statistics, so I can't provide numerical analysis, but I spoke with Joanne, and I talked to four account managers, and they all agree it is a good idea."

Lily (Kate's manager): "Ok, how can we get a hold of the usage stats to corroborate your anecdotal evidence?"

Kate: "I'm not sure. I'm not convinced we have the right numbers, or at least they aren't in the right format. I've asked IT to send me new numbers, but I haven't heard back yet."

Kate (to Lily's manager, Lev): "Hey, Lev. I've talked to loads of customers and colleagues, and I think that we should add this new feature."

Lev: "Fabulous. What does Lily say? Are we adding it?"

Kate: "Well, Lily wants to wait until we have usage stats, but IT haven't come back to me. I am confident it is the right thing to do. Most of our customers want this new feature. We might lose those customers if we wait around for numbers. I say we go for it."

Lev: "Ok, I'll talk to Lily and see if we can get aligned."

In both scenarios, unless Lev really knows Kate and Dave, and understands the full context of what is happening, he is likely to, perhaps inadvertently, pressure Lily into accepting a half-informed decision. That conversation might look something like this:

Lev: "Hey, Lily, sounds like we have a great feature in the works. What's the hold up?"

Lily now feels like she might be the hold up, and doesn't want to disappoint her boss, Lev. So, she replies, "Well, I just think we need a bit more information before we can make a good decision."

Lev doesn't really understand what Lily means but is impatient for a decision. He shakes his head in frustration, "Ok, well, get what you need together and get that decision made." Lev inherently wants to support Lily and appreciates that the right decision will come from fully informed analysis. However, that isn't how his comment comes across in the moment. Lily feels under pressure to provide a decision – any decision. She is therefore more likely to let an ill-considered decision pass, rather than insisting they keep going until all relevant information is considered.

Dave and Kate stay in their respective comfort zones, and Joanne gets what she wants. But was it the right decision? Is this where Acme should be spending resources? Lily would ideally explain to Lev that she is trying to push Dave and Kate to broaden their skills. She wants to make sound product decisions based both on personal inputs, data, and a solid business case that considered the opportunity cost of building this enhancement. However, that requires a fair effort on Lily's part. She will need to invest time and show great patience to shift behavior in her team.

If Lily is not too bothered about how the decision is made, she'll take Kate or Dave's half-informed analysis, and allow the decision to be made based on partial information. Let's say Lily feels very strongly Dave's analysis needs to be supplemented by actual feedback from customers and colleagues. She can do one of two things: talk to the customers and colleagues herself or keep pushing Dave to do it. Her choice here very likely depends on *Lily's* comfort zone. If Lily is people-focused, she may very well go and talk to the relevant people that can inform the decision herself. If she is analytical, she may be slightly more likely to lean on Dave to step out of his comfort zone. That being said, though, there will be a logical, and likely subconscious, analysis of trade-offs happening in Lily's head. Lily decides how to proceed based on a number of factors:

> **Factor 1**: The path of least resistance. Which causes less friction: nagging Dave or doing Dave's job for him? If Lily is conflict-averse and Dave is stubborn, Lily will do Dave's job for him. She will convince herself that it's faster and more efficient if she just does it. She can also tell herself she'll do a better job at it than Dave, because she is more of a people-person. She might be right.

**Factor 2**: Time allocation. Which takes less time: nagging Dave, or doing Dave's job for him? Here, time is split into two elements: time spent working and time spent waiting. It may take Lily eight hours to speak to customers, and that eight hours might be spread over five working days as she contacts people and waits for them to respond. But she might wait fifteen working days for Dave to spend eight hours talking to customers and colleagues. Dave is less likely to have the relationships with customers and less likely to actively chase people for responses, given that Dave is not as people-focused as Lily is.

**Factor 3**: Pressure. Where is the pressure on Lily? Does the decision need to happen quickly? Is there pressure from Lily's leadership team to progress this? Is there time on the roadmap in the near future? Lily might be more likely to do Dave's job for him if a decision is needed quickly.

**Factor 4**: Discount applied to the future. How much does Lily discount her investment in Dave's future? We all discount the future in favor of the present. Lily may rationally understand that the best way to help Dave grow into a better product manager is to sit on his shoulders until he gathers all the relevant information and makes an informed decision. This will serve Dave, Lily, and the company better in the long-run. However, she may be discounting the future to such a degree that this factor is rendered irrelevant.

On balance, people are unlikely to change the way they behave, unless they are pushed to do so. It is time-consuming for managers to accomplish this. Most people follow the path of least resistance, and behavior patterns remain unchanged. Most product decisions are unduly influenced by the strengths and weaknesses of the people making the decisions. The simplest fix is to only employ product managers who have well-rounded comfort zones in both people skills and analytics. However, this is virtually impossible. So, a reasonable second alternative is to pair up product managers with opposing skills and incentivize them to collaborate effectively.

Lily: "Dave, Kate – I want the two of you to work on a decision regarding Joanne's feedback. Dave, you pull together analysis of the relevant usage metrics. Kate, get on the phone with Joanne and a few other account managers and figure out what she is trying to achieve with this enhancement request. Find out if other customers want it. When you two have pulled this all together, you can present it to me and the team at our next team meeting. From there we can decide if we want to take it forward or not."

In this scenario, Lily is more likely to get the relevant input she needs to ensure the team make a good decision about Joanne's feedback. We are stepping out of the traditional hierarchical approach to team organization and moving toward a skill-based fluidity of aligning needs to capabilities. Dave is capable of carrying out usage analysis. Kate is capable of meeting customers and colleagues. He has the analytical skills; she has the relationships. Together, they build a business case based on their collective research. It is then Lily's job to challenge that business case.

There are some fundamental questions any high-performing team should consider before submitting to senior leadership. You can think of it like a business case pre-flight checklist:

1. Have we collected all relevant data that will inform our decision?

2. Have we spoken to a representative sample of users affected by the proposed enhancement?

3. Have we leveraged these inputs in putting together a full business case?

4. If we expect additional revenue, is there a sales plan agreed for how to capture that revenue?

5. What would we be doing with the required resources if we didn't spend time on this enhancement?

Once these questions are addressed, Lily feels more confident that both qualitative and quantitative angles were considered in the preparation of making a decision, which puts the team in a strong position.

This anecdote relates to one tiny piece of feedback, from one customer, at a company that has hundreds of thousands of customers across several working divisions. It is not reasonable to expect Lily and her team to conduct the level of analysis described above for every enhancement request. Lily must find a way to ensure her team stays focused on the enhancement requests that are worth investigating. This means the majority of requests will be disqualified immediately by Chief Poo-Poo Officers. Lily and her team can only spend time evaluating product enhancement requests that are aligned to the product strategy and therefore warrant attention.

# Key Takeaways

- Customer feedback should not go into a black hole. It is important that discrete decisions are made to determine if feedback will result in action, and those decisions should be communicated back to customers.

- Financial performance is a lagging indicator of product suitability, particularly in subscription businesses.

- When evaluating product feedback, individual preferences result in biased conclusions.

- Good product decisions rely on both qualitative and quantitative investigation.

# CHAPTER 10

# Products Don't Sell Themselves

Most products fail to achieve financial success. I am therefore skeptical of any silver bullet process, method, or algorithm that will guarantee success when it comes to selling products, especially at a chunky corporate. The many books that claim to reveal how to build products that sell themselves target entrepreneurs and startups for a reason. Chunky corporates are different beasts. The size of a chunky corporate creates internal competition for product focus because chunky corporates have many products to sell to customers. Therefore, chunky corporate product managers must vie for time with customers to make their products successful. Who controls the time with customers? The sales team. So, if a product manager seeks commercial success for her product line, she must reach customers via the sales team. The first sale of any new product is internal. Product managers must convince the sales team a new product is worth selling.

A manager of mine once said to me, "Salespeople are opportunistic learners." He meant that salespeople learn about products when they need to know about them – not before. With many more years under my belt, I would say all people are opportunistic learners. We are inundated with more information than we could possibly take in at any given point in time. Therefore, we ignore superfluous information until it becomes relevant. Salespeople are pulled in a thousand different directions at a typical chunky corporate. Corporate environments are large and sophisticated. Salespeople are specialized and aligned to specific products and/or regions. Sales teams are also regularly reorganized either because of acquisitions or poor performance. Chunky corporate salespeople get used to constantly changing territories and shifting product focus. The only real constant for sales teams at chunky corporates is the pressure to deliver new deals and growth.

In contrast, most lean startups don't have a sales team. They primarily rely on engines of growth based in customer behavior and direct marketing. Or they rely on their founders and leaders to act as salespeople and land the big deals. Chunky corporate sales teams, in contrast, each have a defined quota and commission plan associated with a specific set of regions and products. Salespeople get more money if they win more deals. Sales commission plans are designed to incentivize closing deals to meet target bookings that consequently form the individual salesperson's quota for the term (a month, a quarter, a year). This method for employing salespeople is effective at driving sales focus. That is the point. Leadership teams want salespeople to remain laser-focused on delivering bookings to the business. That focus comes to the detriment of new product opportunities. Execution not innovation isn't just a mantra for product people at a chunky corporate. It extends to the sales team, too. Did anybody ever explain that to product team, though?

When the product team was hiring product managers, I doubt they said to prospective job candidates: "So the last thing we want you to do is roll out new products. It will be a waste of time because our sales incentive structures aren't designed to push new products. We encourage salespeople to sell what they know." I've certainly never had that conversation in a job interview. What is much more common is that optimistic product managers work really hard to get new products built. Then they work really hard to get the attention of the sales team long enough to train them on the new products. Next they sit back and watch the sales team ignore the new products in favor of selling the old stuff. When product managers are held to account for not delivering on the airtight business case they presented to leadership promising growth from the new product, they blame sales. Then everybody looks awkwardly around the room and wonders what went wrong.

They were doomed from the start. Their leadership team did not put the right structure in place to enable a successful product launch. Everyone assumed the product would be so good it would sell itself. Years of experience have shown me that they rarely sell themselves. You can have the best product in the world, and if no one knows about it, it won't make a dime. If you have achieved a green light from your leadership team to build a new product, that is a huge win in itself. The last thing you want is for it to fall over at the last hurdle.

## Why Can't I Get Sales' Attention?

It takes a newly hired salesperson a good few months to get up to speed on the products, build a pipeline, and start closing deals. Successful salespeople maintain a healthy pipeline of opportunities aligned to the products the salesperson knows best. These should also be the products against which the salesperson has dedicated quota. So what happens when a new product is introduced? Most of the time: nothing. But why? Why do most products fail? Is it because the product team built the wrong thing? Sometimes. However, products often fail because the sales team is not focused on selling it. If a salesperson does not have dedicated quota against a new product, the product is more likely to fail. With the same quota and more products to choose from, we create a zero-sum game. If the salesperson sells the new product in hitting her quota, she naturally sells less of the old. The only scenario in which we have appropriate incentives to sell both new and old products is if the pie gets bigger: bigger quota.

Put yourself in the shoes of a typical salesperson at Acme, Phillip, who has a set of target customers carefully curated for the purposes of selling the core product offering. In this case that core offering is an annual subscription to an online database which costs $20,000/year and provides geospatial aerial satellite imagery. Phillip gets commission for every subscription he sells. After the first month of subscription, Phillip hands the account over to a team of account managers tasked with retaining and growing accounts. Phillip knows the aerial imagery product well. It is proven in the marketplace with a mature customer base.

A product manager comes along and gives Phillip training on a new product that is going to be launched in the next few months. The product offers access to a new database offering ground-based imagery, and it costs $10,000/year. The product manager assumes Phillip will sell this product with the same vigor as he sells the aerial imagery products he already knows. But why would Phillip do that? He doesn't know this product as well (despite training). He has a product manager telling him how great it will be for his customers to be able to purchase both aerial and ground imagery, but Phillip has been warming his customers up for a $20,000 spend, not $30,000.

Introducing the new product could slow down Phillip's existing deals. Phillip worries that customers may not want to buy it. He fears it will be a waste of time to discuss it with prospective customers, and it might even put sales of the satellite imagery product at risk. Phillip figures it is safer to sit back and see if anyone else starts to generate bookings of the new product before pushing it in his carefully curated lists of prospects. And there you have it. If most salespeople react to new product releases in the way outlined above, the product is doomed. Members of the sales team don't have any incentive to sell a new product.

People are not necessarily comfortable or excited to learn new things in the context of chunky corporate world; they are incentivized against strict execution of things they know. Salespeople will (quite rightly) take the low-risk option when building a pipeline and generating bookings. Their incentive structures are designed to maximize bookings of any product they can sell, and they will therefore choose the lowest risk product to pitch to customers. The lowest risk product in each salesperson's mind is the one she understands the best. This is where we get to the opportunistic learners part. If your salespeople cannot see the opportunity associated with the new product, they have no incentive to learn about it. Put plainly, by the immortal words of Homer Simpson: "Besides, every time I learn something new, it pushes some old stuff out of my brain. Remember when I took that home wine-making course, and I forgot how to drive?"

Why would an established salesperson dedicate brain space to an unproven risky product? Phillip would have to divert his attention from closing deals on the aerial imagery product in order to learn about ground imagery products. If Phillip's quota is set to the appropriate amount, Phillip risks missing his targets by taking the time to learn a new product. Any diversion of his time and resources limits his ability to hit maximum quota. If Phillip sells less than his quota, company revenue is impacted, and margins are diluted. If Phillip sells less than his quota, he doesn't get his bonus or an invite to the company's success conference in Hawaii. Phillip does not risk that consequence lightly.

Phillip's quota is $500,000 bookings a year. He needs to close twenty-five aerial imagery deals at the full price of $20,000 to meet his quota. He has a strong pipeline of seventy-five qualified leads to chase. If ten of those leads decide to purchase the ground imagery product for $10,000 instead of the $20,000 aerial imagery product, that creates a $100,000 hole in Phillip's quota. When Phillip discusses the combined product for $30,000 with customers in his pipeline, the additional budget delays the purchase process, making it harder for Phillip to hit is quota in the current period. Plus, Phillip doesn't know the ground imagery product as well. When he pitches it to customers, they ask him questions he can't answer. He spends time getting questions answered, reducing the amount of time he can spend working his carefully curated list of seventy-five opportunities. After a few tentative steps, Phillip decides that pushing the new product is just too risky. He reverts to the plan he knows: work his seventy-five opportunities to hit his quota. Maybe he can focus on the new product next year.

Now let's look at the launch of ground imagery from a product perspective, rather than a sales perspective. The product leader, Carmen, has been working for months getting the ground imagery product off the ground. Six months ago she presented a business case to the senior leadership team demonstrating market demand for ground imagery. She has priced it attractively, much lower than other products, in an effort to build product momentum at launch. She has a product bookings target of $100,000 in year one. She thinks this is really achievable and conservative: the sales team only need to sell ten subscriptions for the new product for Carmen to hit her goal.

However, the overall sales quota is still the same as it was when the budget was set, that is, around the time Carmen wrote her business case. The $100,000 she has projected in sales for the new product is not explicitly reflected in any sales quota. Instead, it is competing with other products for sales attention. As we have demonstrated above, salespeople have no incentive to prioritize new or risky products over the ones they know well. So, in absence of there being a dedicated salesperson tasked with delivering $100,000 of ground imagery revenue, the sales team will stay focused on achieving quota the way they planned to when they were assigned the quota in the first place.

Ensuring that a new product will achieve sales success requires appropriate motivation and incentives. Product managers and business leaders must be acutely aware of the risks associated with new product release. An opportunity cost is an economic term used to describe the potential benefits lost when one makes a choice between alternatives. If I cannot have both option Y and Z, and I choose option Y, then Z is the opportunity cost of choosing option Y. There is an opportunity cost associated with releasing new products: the time salespeople spend selling new products (option Y) could have been spent delivering existing quota (option Z). As team members come up the learning curve, selling new products is slower than selling established products. Therefore, option Y is, at least for a short time, margin diluting as compared to option Z. For option Y to be worthwhile, the leadership team will have to find ways to de-risk the learning curve associated with a new product.

If the team can prove that the new product will give Phillip a chance to beat his quota, not miss his quota, it will get his attention. If a new product provides Phillip with an opportunity, rather than a risk, he is more likely to invest time and resource into learning and pitching it. There are multiple ways to do this. Short-term methods include higher commission rates for the new product over a short period of time, or competitions in which the first salesperson to close a deal on the new product gets a prize. By their nature, these sorts of incentives are unsustainable. If you get lucky and hit the right market at the right time, a new product may, in fact, fly off the shelves. However, this is incredibly rare. Most of the time successful product launches are underpinned by a carefully calculated sales plan and dedicated sales resources.

Acme can offer individual salespeople product-specific quotas at preferential commission rates to incentivize them to sell the ground imagery product. Dedicated quota is the best way for product managers to achieve sales focus and secure a decent shot at new product success. This is not without risk, however. If the product is a flop, the salespeople who had quota against it will suffer. But if the product starts to get traction among those with a dedicated quota, Acme could see a positive feedback loop develop that creates an engine of growth. Sales momentum gathers when a product connects to the market need via a knowledgeable and capable sales team focused on selling that product. From there, other salespeople will follow their peers and create a positive feedback loop that reinforces success. This momentum could propel the product to the top of the market. Once you reach the top, though, you become a target. The game changes, and you find yourself fending off competitors in a bid to stay there.

# Getting to the Top Is Easier than Staying There

The chunky corporate is usually the incumbent in a market. It's like being a top-ranked tennis player returning for the season with a target on your back. Everybody wants to be number one. The longer you are on top, the harder it is stay there. CEO Blake has found himself competing with lean startups who have the freedom of fluid roadmaps. He sees them nipping at his heels, stealing customers who have grown disgruntled with Acme Tech. One morning, Blake awakes to an email from one of his account managers, Gail, sent late the previous evening: "We just received a cancellation notification from Aurora, Inc. They have decided to move to GS Surveys." Blake is incensed.

GS Surveys is a startup founded by Casey McNamara. Casey was a sales manager in Acme Corp's Survey Division before Blake let him go about eighteen months ago. Blake reacts emotionally. He says the word "asshole" out loud and finds himself irrationally angry with Casey. He makes himself a cup of coffee and stews on the prospect of his former colleague stealing his customers. Then he thinks to himself, "Oh, please, there is no way GS Surveys, who only started operating twelve months ago, can truly be a threat. Casey isn't capable of building a platform that could possibly compete with what we've had decades to build."

Blake starts to research GS Surveys online. He sees that Casey has been picking off resources from Acme Tech over the last twelve months. He's hired a database engineer and a mid-level manager that Acme let go. GS have built an MVP that can compete with Acme, and it exploits the weaknesses in Acme's products. What Blake doesn't know is that Casey has contacted the top five customers of Acme's Survey Division that he knows are disgruntled with Acme's software platform. He offers them a shiny new alternative, built entirely to exploit Acme's weaknesses. What Casey knows hasn't hit Blake yet: starting over is sometimes easier than managing change.

Let's carry on with the metaphor of the Joneses building a house from Chapter 1. Blake thinks the Joneses will never move into *just a living room* when they have a *whole house* in Acme's Survey platform. But Casey isn't selling them a house. He is selling them a different idea. Casey comes to them with a slick, brand-new camper van (one of the cool electric VW ones, not the recreational vehicle type that old people use for touring). It is mobile, compact, and not exactly a house, but it is modern and fun. It fundamentally offers them all that they need to solve business problems. Casey sells the Joneses on the dream of travel: the grass could, in fact, be greener somewhere out there. It's a long shot, but if the Joneses are feeling overwhelmed by the amount of maintenance a whole house takes, they might just take the plunge with Casey. The painful irony of this situation is that the Joneses are very unlikely to buy a camper van from Acme because Acme is in the house-building business.

More than once in my career I have had the experience of being disrupted by a smaller, leaner, and less mature software startup. I'll be honest. In these scenarios, it feels a bit like the startup is cheating. You proved there was a market years ago and assume that gives you the right to own it today. But here come the disruptors, learning from your mistakes, and doing what you do, only better. You feel betrayed by your former colleagues, and it is incredibly frustrating to watch another company with fewer resources eat your lunch. It is painful to realize how much easier it is to build a new platform than migrate customers from one existing platform to another one. Disruption is part of doing business, though, and competition from smaller, leaner organizations requires chunky corporates to keep on top of what customers care about.

When the disruptors come, a chunky corporate needs to know exactly what territory it is willing to concede and for what territory it is willing to fight. First, let's look at the market conditions that make disruption likely. The most obvious factor is growth rate. Markets experiencing double-digit growth are common targets for startups. A high growth rate indicates excess demand, and it is an easy place for new entrants to grow a customer base. Next, let's review the circumstances that make a mature organization vulnerable to being disrupted. If relationships with customers are strong, and the software platform is performing, then a disruptor will have limited success enticing Acme's customers to leave. However, if, on the other hand, Acme's platform is outdated and its customer relationships are strained or weak, Acme will likely lose customers to lean startups that see that combination as an opportunity.

One of the more painful disruption types I've encountered is watching a group of colleagues leave my chunky corporate, build a simpler, less feature-rich tool around a particular pain point they know the chunky corporate cannot accommodate, and pick off customers one by one. In fact, it is a logical outcome of specific forces governing a market and an organization. We've seen the emotional pain it causes Blake. Now, let's put ourselves into the shoes of one of Blake's team members.

Juan manages the development team in Acme's Survey Division. The team maintains an aging platform that delivers online survey tools. Juan hears from the account management team that Survey Division's software is slow and manual. It doesn't have all the whizzy search features and automatic population of data that users expect these days.

As an example, Survey Division's platform doesn't save your profile when you complete a survey, so you have to re-enter your preferences every time you log in. These features were not common when Survey Division built its platform years ago, but, today, they are table stakes. The sales team feel somewhat embarrassed when attempting to sell the Survey Division platform to new customers. New customers expect these sorts of features, and the lack of them makes Survey Division's platform look antiquated.

Juan, being a former developer and having a deep knowledge of the way Survey Division's platform works, knows the underlying software needs rebuilding. There is no easy way to retrofit modern features into the existing application. He feels the pressure and is being pulled in a thousand different directions. He does not have the tools to manage competing priorities of customers, sales colleagues, marketing, and product. It feels to Juan like all of these stakeholders are shouting at him to go faster, deliver more, and be more agile, but none of them understand how complicated and archaic the underlying software is.

If they knew what he was dealing with: a mountain of tech debt and impossible enhancement requests, they would know they are setting him up for failure. Juan doesn't even have time to prioritize requests effectively. He is simply treading water, trying his best to keep his head above the waves in a sea of expectations. Without strong product leadership, he delivers features based on whomever is shouting the loudest at any given point in time. If he focuses development effort on replatforming the product stack, Acme will keep losing customers as the legacy platform underperforms. If he continues working on the legacy platform, replatforming takes longer. Juan feels exhausted. He is doing his best but is hopeless about the prospects of ever digging out of his current software development hole. After slogging away in this sort of working environment, Juan is approached by his former colleague, Casey. Casey empathizes with Juan's frustration and offers an attractive alternative.

Casey: "Juan, I totally get it. They don't appreciate you. The guys in headquarters don't pay enough attention to Survey Division, and they don't realize that customer frustrations are growing. But I get it. I've been out of Acme for six months now, and I can see that the market is changing. Customers don't care as much about the big, bulky features that Survey Division built years ago. They just want that slick user experience. If we build something light, modern and tailored to our customers' needs, we could entice disgruntled Acme customers to buy from us. And you are just the man to build it. How does Chief Technology Officer of GS Surveys sound?"

Juan: "Wow, thanks for considering me, Casey. I don't know. I always thought really highly of the leadership team at Survey Division and Acme Tech as a whole. It feels like I might betray them if I build a competitive offering. Plus, I have a non-compete in my contract."

Casey: "I felt that way, too, Juan. And then they let me go. You know what I learned about Acme Tech? They don't care about you. They have no loyalty to you. You are just a number to them. You need to put yourself first. No one else will. This is just the way the game works. I mean, when was the last time Acme gave you the resources you need to deliver a high-quality product? When was the last time they gave you a substantial pay rise? They don't value you. I will value you. As CTO, you have a chance to propel your career to the next level. I will give you equity in the company, so that when we are successful competitors of Acme, you can share in the rewards."

Juan: "Hmmm. Maybe." In his head, Juan thinks, *I do feel ignored and undervalued most of the time. I am just a mid-level employee. I don't even think Blake knows my name. Maybe this is the right time to take a risk and go somewhere I will get the recognition I deserve.*

Casey: "Now you are talking. If your non-compete was anything like mine, it will bar you from working at a competitor for six months. So, you can take some time off and come to work for me just as the product build starts to ramp up."

Fast forward twelve months and Casey and Juan have launched an MVP with a flagship customer, Aurora Inc., while Acme is in the throes of a difficult replatforming project in Survey Division. It wasn't hard for Casey to convince Aurora to leave. Their Survey Division accounts manager, Gail, was on his team when he worked at Acme. She was always complaining to him about how high maintenance Aurora was as a customer and how Juan was never quick enough to respond to their requests for additional software features. All Casey had to do was reach out to the point of contact at Aurora and tell him about this new shiny product that is better than Acme's in multiple ways. Casey is incredibly familiar with Acme's pricing and offers Aurora a better deal.

What has Aurora got to lose? Because Aurora is GS's first (and only) customer, Juan can be completely dedicated to making sure Aurora feels special in their first year with GS. Juan can adjust the product roadmap as needed to keep Aurora happy. With the Aurora testimonial backing them up, GS is now in a decent position to start picking off other customers from Acme. Before long, other disgruntled colleagues from Acme's Survey Division start proactively reaching out to Casey to see if there might be job opportunities for them at GS.

Meanwhile, Blake is reeling. He cannot help but feel personally betrayed by Casey and Juan. He feels compelled to react. He speaks to his legal team about whether or not Casey or Juan have breached the terms of their departures from Acme. He whips the Survey Division sales team into a frenzy to go and protect customers. He rants at the head of Survey Division's technology development team: "Go faster. Do better. Be more agile when faced with customer requests. Launch the new platform." Blake is mad. His ego is bruised and he is acting in frustration and anger. It feels personal to him. He feels threatened by GS.

Those feelings flow from Blake to his team and kick off a cascade of fight or flight emotions across Survey Division. They feel Blake's anger and perceive GS as a competitive threat. Logically, we can look at this situation and see that the calm and reasonable thing to do would be to take a step back. Take a deep breath. Identify at-risk customers and invest in strengthening relationships with them by listening to their pain points. Determine if addressing these pain points fits into the replatforming strategy for Acme's Survey Division. If they do, make them high priority in the replatforming project and stay laser focused on delivering the plan. If they do not fit into the overall product strategy, and that strategy remains sound, then make a plan for how the sales team can offset the revenue losses of customers that will logically move across to GS.

While it is natural to have an emotional reaction to discovering Casey and Juan are actively targeting both his customers and his colleagues, Blake cannot let that emotion influence his course of action. He cannot let his team get so focused on crushing GS that they lose sight of Survey Division's goals. It doesn't matter whether GS was founded by ex-Acme staff or complete newcomers. GS is simply a market competitor, and part of doing business is insulating against competition. Blake should be focused on staying competitive more broadly, not just crushing GS. There is an opportunity cost associated with spending too much resource targeting a single competitor. Blake is human, and he is entitled to having a human reaction. With a strong team around him, though, he can see reason and not let his emotional reaction impact business performance.

What can Blake do to avoid disruption by new market entrants? As with anything, an ounce of prevention is worth a pound of regret. The best way to avoid disruption is to keep your product and customer relationships strong. That, however, is easier said than done when you have cost-conscious investors to satisfy. Most chunky corporates don't start improving products until the existing product set has become outdated, and Acme Tech is no exception. From there, the question becomes: can you improve your products fast enough to prevent disruptors from having a material impact on your business?

# Responding to External Threats

There are a number of factors that make a chunky corporate more resilient against external threats:

1.  Your sales team has strong relationships with its customers and can proactively identify accounts at risk.

2.  Your product team is closely watching competitive evolutions.

3.  Your product strategy is well-defined.

4.  Members of both the sales and product teams understand the market in which you have a right to win.

It would be easy for Acme to feel threatened by the departure of Aurora. If Aurora is leaving Acme because it has not delivered on table-stakes features, then Acme needs to get its act together and improve the product offering. But if Aurora has left Acme because what Aurora wants from the product is not aligned to Acme's product strategy, Acme should let Aurora go. If the product strategy is sound, the demand it is designed to capture should outweigh individual account losses resulting from divergence between customer need and product delivery. If Blake's anger prevents him from clearly separating fair customer losses – a result of misalignment between customer need and product delivery – from customer losses that are due to an uncompetitive product offering in the core market, he can very quickly derail Survey Division's product strategy. Blake needs his VP of Product for Survey Division, Lev, to guide him in either scenario.

# Scenario 1: Wet Lettuce Product Leader

Blake: "Lev, what is the deal with GS Survey's product? How can we stay competitive and win back Aurora?"

Lev: "I don't know, Blake. Honestly, this is the first I've heard of any of this. Gail said nothing about Aurora being at risk. I had no idea they were unhappy with the product. Our account managers have got to start feeding this stuff back to me sooner."

Blake: "Right, we have got to win them back. I can't let Casey get the better of us. I mean, I let him go because he isn't that great of a sales leader. Surely he can't win customers off of us!"

Lev: "Definitely. He is completely reactive to customers. He'll be promising them all sorts that Juan will never be able to deliver."

Blake: "How is the product holding up, though? Do you feel good about the replatforming project and our roadmap for enhancements?"

Lev: "Well, we never have enough resources. We are bogged down with replatforming the core platform and it won't be ready for Aurora to use for at least another year. If it were up to me, we'd be looking at artificial intelligence plugins to automatically populate surveys. But we never have time to work on new features because we are always battling with technical debt."

Blake: "We aren't made of money, Lev. We have a strict budget for replatforming. We can't get distracted by big features like AI."

Lev: "I know. I know. But I just can't see how we are going to win back Aurora if we don't add new features."

Lev does not have a clearly nor tightly defined product strategy. He does not have a grip on the competitive market. He does not understand where the boundaries of Survey Division's right to win are. He is all over the place. He is quick to blame the account manager for not telling her that Aurora was at risk. He is quick to blame the development team for not being able to deliver all he wants to accomplish. He has wild, big ideas about how to improve the product, but they are not related to why Aurora left. Lev is guessing. Lev is grasping at straws to hide his own ignorance.

# Scenario 2: Misaligned Customer Need

Blake: "Lev, what is the deal with GS Survey's product? How can we stay competitive and win back Aurora?"

Lev: "Well, frankly, Aurora have been asking us to build features for years now that are simply out of line with the product strategy. Gail and I have looked at their requested enhancements, and they aren't looking for a survey tool. They want a fully customized piece of software that will execute their company-specific workflows. They really should be building their own internal platform. What they want from the product is not what our other customers want from the product. It will take over our product roadmap and cost us more than we make from them if we customize the offering in the way they want."

Blake: "Ugh. So you are telling me we need to let them go. Well, that leaves a $200,000/year gap in the budget."

Lev: "On the upside, if GS Surveys are taking them on as a client, at least we know Juan will be so busy delivering on their custom requirements, he'll struggle to build a scalable repeatable product, and that will limit his ability to compete with us on the whole."

Blake: "Ok, ok. Let me speak to the sales team about how we are going to plug this gap in the budget. We are going to have to sign multiple new customers, and quickly, to make up the shortfall."

Lev: "In the meantime, I'm not giving up on Aurora. The best way to mitigate the risk of them leaving is to have an honest conversation about the requested enhancements we can accommodate and the ones we won't. If we are proactive, maybe we can get them to continue to use us for their core survey requirements. We can possibly introduce them to a partner software company that sells custom software. Perhaps we can salvage some of the relationship that way."

Lev recognizes that Aurora's requests for enhancements are misaligned with the product strategy for Survey Division. He is strong enough to recommend that they let Aurora go and double down on the core market where Survey Division has a right to win.

## Scenario 3: Product Requires Improvement

Blake: "Lev, what is the deal with GS Survey's product? How can we stay competitive and win back Aurora?"

Lev: "Frankly, their product is pretty impressive. I mean, it doesn't have all of the rich features that we have, but it offers a really slim and light version of our core workflows."

Blake: "So, how to we get our product to a place that it can compete?"

Lev: "We have to get this replatforming project on track and delivering working software. It will take the better part of a year, if not more, but by proactively communicating with our customers, particularly those at risk, we can hopefully hold off GS Tech until customers are live in the new platform."

Blake: "Ok. This doesn't change our strategy; we just have to stay completely disciplined in delivering it. I'll coordinate with sales on pulling together a list of customers ranked by risk so we can build a communication plan."

The critical thing that enables Blake to have this last conversation with Lev is his knowledge of the market and the customer base. Lev has a strong product vision and the confidence to say no to customers that are asking Acme to deliver products outside of its core strengths. With this guidance, Blake can put his emotions to one side and see reason.

An efficient response to disruption depends on having a strong product leader whose judgment and assessment of the situation are sound. Sadly, what is much more common in chunky corporates is that Lev is a bit of a wet lettuce (Scenario 1) and just does what Blake tells him to do. Disruption from competitors will put greater pressure on Acme to rebuild portions of its Survey Division product stack. In order to stay competitive, Acme must improve its product offering. Executing this successfully depends on Lev understanding the competitive market, identifying the features that will keep Acme competitive as well as the ones that are now obsolete. Lev and his team must choose the right features to build (or rebuild) to deliver steady financial performance for Acme.

# Key Takeaways

- Dedicated sales resources and specified quota give new products a greater chance of success.

- Disruptors can exploit product weaknesses and disgruntled customers.

- Responding to disruptors effectively requires strong customer relationships, knowledgeable product leaders, and focused execution of product improvements.

# CHAPTER 11

# Good Communication Leads to Good Products

We all know the old adage, right? When you assume, you make an "ass" out of "u" and "me." Nothing derails an Agile project faster than gaps in communication. And after many years of analyzing where communication went wrong, I found a common culprit at the heart of most communication disasters: assumptions. Oh, the little beasts – they creep in where you least expect them, and they color our interpretation of just about everything. Human brains are assumption machines. It is what we do; it is at the heart of how our brains function efficiently. The more you know, the more assumptions you make. Your subconscious starts to take over, and you jump to conclusions based on previous knowledge before you even realize you've done it.

> *It ain't what you don't know that gets you into trouble. It's what you know for sure that just ain't so.*
>
> —Mark Twain

In the context of a Lean-Agile project, we find potential gaps in communication all over the place due to the number of handovers between the various players involved in a project. The larger the team, the

K. Tamblin, *The Lean-Agile Dilemma*, https://doi.org/10.1007/979-8-8688-0321-5_11

more opportunities for gaps. Therefore, a chunky corporate is more likely to struggle with communication gaps as compared to a lean startup. First, a product manager outlines a high-level business plan, based on a set of features. Those features go to a product owner to write requirements. The product owner consults information architects, technical architects, the product manager, and the engineering team's scrum master to document the detailed requirements needed to deliver the features. We are already talking about a minimum of five people who are providing input to the requirements. Requirements are documented as features and user stories in an online development platform, like Azure DevOps, Jira, or Gitlab. The purpose of these platforms is to foster clear communication through common processes. But writing it down doesn't mean the players are aligned or clear on what the words mean.

Each of these five players comes to the collaboration table with a set of assumptions they don't even realize they have. For example, the product manager has assumptions about the best way to deliver the solution, which informs how she writes the business case and describes the features. The product owner has assumptions about what the business is trying to achieve. The technical architect has assumptions about what user scenarios are most important. The information architect has assumptions about data usage. The scrum master has assumptions about how it will be coded, which influences the interpretation of requirements. If these players are not fully aligned on the assumptions, there is a high probability the software will not perform as intended. Usually, colleagues are not aware of how their assumptions influence their decisions. Where assumptions are not identified and validated, there is high likelihood of the resulting software having gaps in design that require additional work, or, even worse, the software might not even deliver what the business needs.

The pursuit of efficiency requires a team of strong, persistent communicators. Effective communication requires clear identification and documentation of assumptions up front. Project teams should be comprised of the technical skills to deliver high-quality work and the communication skills to deliver it efficiently. That said, it is no good communicating bad decisions. So, let's add a third string to our bow. Strong software development teams need a mix of technical skills, communication skills, and good judgment. Hundreds of important decisions are made every day in a software build. Making good ones can be the difference between success and failure.

Are you confident your team knows which decisions they should make on their own and which ones they should escalate? If so, what gives you that confidence? Have you discussed it with your team? Is it written down somewhere? Do you regularly revisit it with your colleagues? If the answer to any of the above questions is no, then there is probably some room for improvement. Every team member has strengths and weaknesses requiring different strategies for helping them to achieve autonomy. Over a beer after a long day of meetings, Blake and I are swapping managerial war stories. I tell him about the time I had a lovely team of people to manage who at the same time as being lovely, were highly frustrating.

On this team, I had two product managers. They each had several years of experience and were roughly on the same level. One, named Otto, had a strong analytical skill set and was still relatively willing to speak to customers when necessary. He approached problems methodically and almost always recommended an appropriate course of action when faced with a challenge. However, Otto lacked confidence in his own ability to make appropriate decisions. He would ask my opinion for nearly every decision he faced. In our one-to-one sessions, I regularly teased him that he was not giving himself enough credit. I praised his abilities and encouraged him (repeatedly) to make decisions without me. It wasn't because I didn't want to help Otto when he was unsure. It was primarily because waiting for a response from me could slow him down. I offered Otto autonomy, but he wasn't confident enough to take it.

In stark contrast to Otto was another product manager on my team, Kirk, who was great with people and loved spending days out with them. He had great relationships with colleagues and customers, and everyone loved Kirk. Kirk, however, struggled with understanding how the underlying technology worked. That made it hard for him to develop a strong gut instinct for what would be easy or hard to build. To him, the software was a magical black box where anything was possible. Kirk had a slightly bad habit of suggesting to customers that we could add wildly unrealistic features to the software, simply because he didn't recognize they were unrealistic.

Kirk had all the confidence, and he never asked my opinion before sending not-entirely-well-considered features into sprint. I laughed as I recollected for Blake how funny it was at the time to be constantly telling Otto to make his own decisions and constantly telling Kirk to stop making decisions without asking my opinion. The moral of the story is that good judgment has two elements:

1. The ability to make a sound decision

2. Knowing when the decision is yours and when it needs to be escalated to leadership

Good judgment is part skill and part confidence. So, how do we manage these infinite combinations of abilities, skills, experience, and confidence that make all of our team members individuals? One thing that helps immensely is having ground rules. These rules should, of course, be adapted to each project and each team, but there are some common ones that serve as a good foundation. These are some of the product decisions that I require be socialized in a stakeholder forum:

# 1. Which Features to Build

The list of features on to the product road map is one of the most important sets of decisions product people make. Once determined, it should then be stored somewhere where stakeholders can access (but not edit) it for reference. Any new feature that the team wants to introduce and any feature that the team proposes should be removed or materially modified must be agreed in the same forum as the original list. This is not something that can be delegated to the point that business leadership loses sight of it.

# 2. What Data to Migrate

When replatforming, there will come a time when someone decides what data can be successfully extracted, transformed, and loaded from the old platforms to the new. This needs to be agreed in a shared forum so that affected stakeholders are well aware of any data changes or data loss they will experience as part of the migration.

# 3. The Product List

We've already discussed the importance of the user-product-package-subscription model. The list of products and packages available for sale and enabled by technology should be agreed by all relevant stakeholders. Changes to this should be socialized in the same forum.

As you have probably noticed, the aim of all of this is to ensure there is appropriate communication among the team when important decisions are made. The team must recognize what constitutes an important decision. By creating repeatable processes and forums for discussing these, team leaders can build clear expectations and avoid mistaken assumptions. Appropriate discussion and guidance from multiple stakeholders when consequential decisions arise improves outcomes.

Blake asks me what I did with my team of funny product managers. "I created a bi-weekly meeting for us to discuss any new products or features with a group of business stakeholders. We called it the Product Working Group (PWG)." Blake and I talk about where, at Acme, these sorts of forums are needed but not happening regularly. I recommend that John implement a weekly design forum in which he can oversee architectural decisions and provide guidance to his technical teams. He can also identify any design elements that might impact business stakeholders, like colleagues in product, data science, or finance teams.

In the design forum, John normalizes the practice of making architectural decisions with input from colleagues that would traditionally not be consulted. Similarly, I recommend that he put in place a regular data forum, with stakeholders from product, data science, and technology coming together to discuss how technology and data can meet the needs of the business. I make a caveat to Blake, though. There is a balance to be struck. We do not want to create meetings for meetings' sake. However, we need to ensure that the sort of collaboration that happens naturally at a Lean Startup is happening at Acme.

Once the processes are in place, key stakeholders know that they will be asked at the appropriate forum about whether or not key decisions included input from relevant stakeholders Hopefully, when collaboration becomes second nature, the meetings themselves become unnecessary. This isn't rocket science, and most teams know the right things to do in order to execute a plan. Where things get all muddled is when the individual players delivering the work lose sight of the big picture, and the managers who are accountable for delivering the big picture lose focus on empowering their teams to accomplish it.

# Be Curious

In any large, mature business, there will be misunderstandings and miscommunications. Inevitably, and probably on a daily basis, colleagues will feel disappointed as a result of a gap between their expectation and reality. *I expected my colleague to ask me what color the new button on the dashboard should be before building it. I never would have picked that shade of green!* The negative emotional reaction to finding that your colleague didn't do what you expected him or her to do is completely natural. That being said, it can become poisonous to an organization when communication and collaboration break down as a result of repeated misalignment between expectations and outcomes.

It comes down to trust and credibility, really. And at the heart of mistrust or misunderstanding is usually poor communication. Whenever I feel myself wanting to judge a colleague for doing something differently to what I would have done, or what I expected, I stop myself and ask more questions. Most of the time, by asking questions, I find that there was logic in my colleague's decision. My colleague may not have come to the same conclusion I would have, but that doesn't mean my colleague is somehow less capable than I am. It doesn't mean my colleague wasn't thinking.

The misalignment between the expected outcome (*what I would have done*) and the actual outcome (*what my colleague did*) usually has to do with a different perspective, a different view of the context, or some false assumptions. It is very rare in my experience that a colleague made a bad decision simply because they didn't think or didn't care. So, if we accept that most of the time disappointment is a result of misunderstanding, rather than a lack of skill or effort, we can reframe our responses to illicit more positive outcomes.

The most common occurrence is that there simply wasn't enough context, communication, or alignment in advance of decisions being made. The number of relationships across which information must flow increases the likelihood of miscommunication or misalignment.

Let's look at an example. Ella is the product owner for Essays Online, part of the Publishing Division at Acme. She participated in the technical design, which includes a customer status reference list, which holds five values: Submitted, Open, Passed, Failed, Closed.

However, when Ella sees the workflow demonstrated in a sprint review, she sees there are two reference lists. List one is Essay Status, with two values: Open and Closed. List two is Essay Result, with three values: Submitted, Passed, and Failed. Essay Status refers to whether or not the essay requires action, and the Essay Result refers to whether or not the essay was sufficient. If the Status is Open, the user could be in the process of submitting, or in the process of having an essay graded. Once the essay has been reviewed and the Essay Result revealed to the user, the Status is closed.

The feature works, but Ella feels aggrieved that the outcome doesn't match the original design. She is frustrated that she wasn't advised or consulted when this change was made and worries it will have unforeseen consequences. Ella negatively judges the actions of the scrum master, Pete, before speaking with him. Ella confronts Pete: "Why did you change one status reference list into two lists?" Pete feels Ella's frustration and responds defensively: "IA told me to." Pete has effectively rid himself of Ella's frustration and absolved himself of responsibility by palming Ella off onto Information Architecture (IA). Ella immediately shifts her negative judgment of the situation from Pete to Julian, the information architect assigned to this feature.

Ella confronts Julian: "Why did you change the design of the reference list from the requirement in the user stories?" Julian senses Ella's frustration and feels the need to justify his actions. He responds defensively: "It didn't make sense to have a single list of statuses. When the essay is Submitted, it is still Open, so you need two separate reference lists so you can see both elements, Submitted and Open, or Failed and Closed, at the same time." Ella isn't convinced by Julian's argument and prefers the original design. She responds: "Yes, but the status Submitted implies the issue is still Open, so having two statuses is redundant." Julian is growing frustrated as well. He feels undermined by Ella's line of questioning. He feels concerned that she does not trust him to be the expert in information design and wants to be right about the design decision he has taken. If he was wrong, it could mean the team has to rebuild the feature. He is struggling to articulate his point of view because his emotions distract him. He is uncomfortable and wants the conversation to end. He says, "That makes the data messy," and walks away.

Ella grows increasingly frustrated. She logs into the test environment to try out the feature. She notices the user interface only displays one data field associated with the status and result of an Essay. Because of the change in reference data, however, there are two important pieces of information pertaining to the essay. Ella doesn't know why Pete chose to display Essay Status instead of Essay Result in the UI, but it means when users log into the portal, they can see if their Essay is Open or Closed, but they can't see if they Passed or not!

Ella knows it will take additional development resources to build the additional field in the user interface. Angrily, Ella walks over to Julian: "Now you've changed it, the summary page doesn't display enough information. It was supposed to show the user if the essay got a passing grade or not, but now all it shows is Open. That doesn't tell the user anything useful!"

Julian realizes there was an unintended consequence in the front-end to the change that he has made in the back-end reference data. He feels some concern that his change was responsible for a poor user experience but quickly pushes that to one side. The user interface is not his area and not his concern. Rather than open up to Ella and try to collaborate to find the best way forward, he remains defensive. He shifts the responsibility back to Ella: "Then we need a new feature to add another data field to the UI to show the customer both statuses. It's a design gap." Ella is now incensed. It is her responsibility to deliver the feature to specification and on time. It is she, as product owner, who will be judged for this additional work, and it will reflect badly on her. Angry, concerned, and feeling decidedly un-collaborative, Ella retorts, "We are already late delivering this feature, and the scrum team is supposed to be working on another epic entirely in the next sprint. When are we going to have time to deliver a new feature to show the additional information to customers?"

Julian walks away and convinces himself this is not his problem. He was just putting the best data design possible forward. He was right to create two statuses. It isn't his fault that the rest of the team didn't think through how the change in data design would impact the user experience. Besides, he has a long list of data designs on his desk for other features that he needs to finish. Ella wants to bang her head into a brick wall multiple times as she considers how she will explain to the project manager and the leadership team that she needs Pete's team to stop working on the new epic they just took into sprint and come back to this one for a few days to make a change.

She can already foresee how this is going to play out. The scrum team will say that adding this additional data field to the UI was not in the original design (therefore a design gap). They will use this label to move this additional feature to the bottom of the list of requested enhancements. Ella wants to call it a bug because it was a result of a design change, not a design gap. The software does not deliver what her feature requires. If it is labelled a bug, the scrum team has to put it into sprint immediately, as the scrum bears responsibility for fixing bugs. However, if it is labeled a design gap, then Ella is responsible for finding time in the sprint plan to get it addressed, and she'll have to write another feature to cover it. Those innocuous words, design gap, are often used to shift blame from the development team to the product owner.

When you hear them used regularly, or when you hear product owners debating with engineers as to whether or not something was a gap or a bug, your product owners and your development teams are not collaborating effectively. It is a symptom of underlying tension. At this point, communication either stops or becomes completely unproductive. No one in this scenario is right or wrong; they just have different perspectives and different objectives. Neither party had full view of the consequences or impact of the decision (one reference list or two) on the other's area of expertise (back-end data or front-end user experience). Julian's top priority is to have clean, structured data in the back-end. Ella's top priority is to have a clear and useful user experience in the front-end. Neither had a full view of the other's perspective before the decision to make a change was made. Her judgment of Julian's actions provokes a defensive response.

In a lean startup, Ella and Julian sit across a table from each other, or in a virtual communication channel, regularly talking about the design and implementation all day every day. As they have a personal relationship, it would be natural for Julian to ask Ella in passing: "Hey, I want to change the single reference list to be two reference lists for these reasons..." to which Ella would have said, "Ok, that's fine, but I'll need to change the UI design to reflect that so it works for the user." They then would have looped in the scrum master: "Hey, Pete, how long would it take to add two status flags to the page instead of one?" They agree, then and there, to make the change, as a collaborative team.

Sadly, in most chunky corporates, these three players, Julian, Ella, and Pete, are in different teams and time zones. Julian is serving multiple scrums, providing designs across lots of different features, and managing lots of spinning plates. It isn't that Julian doesn't want to tell Ella about the change. Perhaps Julian assumed Pete would tell Ella. Or maybe he just didn't think it was important. Thousands of unimportant decisions are made like this during large software projects, and most of them have unintended consequences. Those unintended consequences are where inefficiency lurks. So, if Ella, Julian, and Pete cannot magically turn back the clock to when the organization was a lean startup, what should they do differently? A good start is for Ella to not interrogate Julian and Pete with judgment. Ella should be curious as to why the change was made, not angry.

Tension escalates via defensive, judgmental reactions. Conversely, tension is diffused by genuine curiosity. So much of the difference between the two is in the subtle starting position of the person asking the questions. I can ask the same question: "Why did you do that?" in a way that sounds like I have already assumed whatever was done was the wrong thing to do. Or I can ask that question slightly differently: "That's an interesting solution. Why did you choose to do it that way?" and get a much more favorable response from my colleague. In the latter of those methods, there is no judgment underlying the question. In fact, it praises the colleague for choosing a unique perspective. Realistically, Ella doesn't know if Julian's decision was right or wrong. Pre-judging serves no purpose. There also is almost never a right or wrong decision in product management, only informed and uninformed decisions. Ella could have asked Julian, gently: "That is an interesting change to the reference lists you've recommended. What is the rationale for having two instead of one?"

Julian: "From a data perspective, these statuses, Submitted, Open, Passed, Failed, and Closed, are really two lists in one."

Ella: "What do you mean?"

Julian: "Well, if the essay has been Submitted, it is also Open. If the essay has Passed or Failed, it is also Closed. So, logically, there should be two lists: Open/Closed, and Submitted/Passed/Failed."

Ella: "Ahh, I see your logic there. Unfortunately, the UI prototype works off of one status, and the reference list it is linked to is Open/Closed, so it doesn't offer the value to the customer that we were hoping for."

Julian: "Oh, I see. Well, could the team just make a small change in the UI to pull from the other reference list, the Submitted/Passed/Failed list in order to achieve that same outcome?"

Ella: "Yes, I think that would work. It's going into sprint in the next few days, though. The team won't be happy with such a last-minute change."

Julian: "Ok, let's talk to Pete and see if he will go with it."

By approaching Julian in a curious and collaborative way, Ella is significantly more likely to get what she wants. Ella is also more likely to keep her cool if this discussion happens before the software is built, not after. She will build a positive, collaborative relationship with Julian, making it less likely for these mishaps to occur in the future. Ideally, the organization wouldn't have to manage communication mishaps. Ideally, the chunky corporate would build cross-functional collaboration into the fabric of the organization.

From the moment colleagues are inducted, they should be bombarded with the expectation that their stakeholders are cross-functional. This way of working must be regularly reinforced until it becomes second nature. Managers must understand the importance of cross-functional collaboration, and they must reinforce it regularly. George, Julian's boss, should consider this when he approves Julian's information design: "Julian, the new design looks great. Have you walked Ella through it yet? Did she have any feedback?"

When managers make this part of the sign-off process, their team members proactively start to emulate it (mostly when they realize the design/feature/code won't be signed off until relevant stakeholders have been consulted). Pete will check with Ella before starting to code: "Ella, have you seen the updated prototype now that IA has changed the reference list? Any issues with the proposed solution?" Ella will give Julian a call as soon as he is assigned to work on the information design of the new feature: "Julian, let me know when you have time for me to walk you through the prototype for essay statuses. It will help inform the underlying data design." Managers must proactively encourage this behavior among their teams. Performance of individuals should be measured against expectations of proactive, assertive, and professional communication with cross-functional stakeholders. Managers and senior leaders must have no tolerance for defensive behavior that escalates negative interactions. They should lead by example and practice de-escalation and calm curiosity when faced with challenging situations. They should equip themselves and their team members with the appropriate situational skills to handle difficult situations with grace.

Communication is intrinsically linked to underlying corporate culture. Ron Westrum has categorized corporate culture into three types: Pathological (power-oriented), Bureaucratic (rule-oriented), and Generative (performance-oriented).[1] Research demonstrates that a culture of psychological safety is predictive of software delivery performance. Software development is a human enterprise, after all. High performance in software delivery is positively associated with the Generative organization typology, as described in Table 11-1.

---

[1] Westrum, Ron. "DevOps Culture: Westrum Organizational Culture," n.d. https://cloud.google.com/architecture/devops/devops-culture-westrum-organizational-cultu.

***Table 11-1.*** *The Westrum organizational typology model*

| Pathological | Bureaucratic | Generative |
|---|---|---|
| Power oriented | Rule oriented | Performance oriented |
| Low cooperation | Modest cooperation | High cooperation |
| Messengers shot | Messengers neglected | Messengers trained |
| Responsibilities shirked | Narrow responsibilities | Risks are shared |
| Bridging discouraged | Bridging tolerated | Bridging encouraged |
| Failure leads to scapegoating | Failure leads to justice | Failure leads to inquiry |
| Novelty crushed | Novelty leads to problems | Novelty implemented |

Westrum's Generative typology creates an environment of psychological safety. Colleagues feel comfortable collaborating, challenging one another, and making mistakes. Managers are well-trained on corporate goals and the methods applied to achieve them. Strong performance is rewarded and individuals are curious, not judgmental, when stakeholders disagree. John, Blake, and I talk about the undercurrents they are observing in cross-team collaboration at Acme. Our discussion turns to where on the corporate culture spectrum Acme sits. Are colleagues working effectively and collaboratively? Or are they fractured and fragmented? Acme wants to be aligned, collaborative, and trusting. However, we are seeing examples of colleagues acting out of fear, retreating into fragmented silos, and not bothering with alignment to the organization's goals. Figure 11-1 demonstrates how an organization can move from negative corporate culture to positive corporate culture through engagement, alignment, and training.

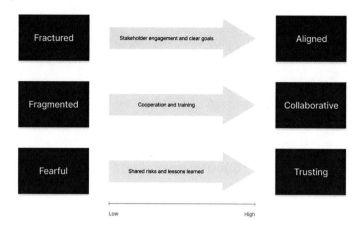

***Figure 11-1.*** *The corporate culture spectrum can be impacted by clear action*

A discussion with Blake and John picks up that tricky task of assessing whether or not teams are aligned around Acme's software goals. "How would you know?" asks Blake. "Oh, you know," says John. "It's obvious when a team is aligned. Our team is completely on board with exactly what needs to be built and how to build it." I raise an eyebrow skeptically before reminding Blake and John about a misalignment I observed recently in Survey Division.

Rafael was the product owner for a milestone whose primary objective was to improve the user experience (UX) of onboarding new customers. At the time, customer onboarding was built into a monolithic platform experience. Users described it as clunky and slow. The UX lead, Tyson, wanted the development team to create a separate application with a new user interface (UI). The technology team agreed that using the existing underlying APIs to deliver information from the database to the new application/new UI would be the fastest way to release it to customers. There were multiple points at which Tyson and Rafael thought the technical design teams, scrum team, and product team were aligned around the business outcome (faster onboarding) and the method (existing APIs, new UI). As the build progressed, they discovered they were not, in fact, as aligned as believed.

Alignment Point A: prepare features for sprint. Rafael writes features dictating the business requirements associated with the new UI. These features describe the new user experience and reference a lovely prototype built by Tyson. When the development team, team Saturn, headed up by scrum master Gretchen, starts building these features, it isn't clear to her the new UI will connect to the existing APIs. Rafael doesn't write anything in the business requirements about the APIs. That is usually the responsibility of the technical architecture team, and Rafael has no visibility into what APIs exist nor what data they carry.

Gretchen and the team make an assumption that since it is a new application, there will be new APIs delivering the appropriate information from the database to the UI. Rafael's features don't reference API design because he expects the existing APIs to stay the same (no design needed). Gretchen's development team assume new APIs will be forthcoming. So, when they are asked to put a "find my address" button on the address entry page, they don't worry that there is no API behind the UI that can carry out that function and search for a user's address. They assume they will be instructed how to connect the new front-end application to the new APIs once they are built, presumably by another team. They focus on building a front-end that looks like the prototype without any curiosity as to how it connects to the back-end. Rafael, Tyson, and Gretchen think they are aligned around building a new application for customer onboarding, but they are not.

Alignment Point B: after the first sprint. Rafael thinks Gretchen and her team are connecting the new UI to existing APIs as they build the front-end. However, in the sprint review, Rafael notices that the UI deviates from what existing APIs can deliver. He worries Gretchen's team is beyond the scope of the project boundaries; he worries about scope creep. He pulls together a meeting with key stakeholders, including me, to agree expectations. In this meeting, we discover that team Saturn's new UI isn't connected to anything.

There is a facade, but with no underlying APIs connected to move data between the facade and the database, it doesn't work. We are astonished. How did Gretchen's team work for two weeks without any engineers asking whether or not the UI should be connected to anything? When questioned about this, Gretchen says, "Last time I refused to take a feature into sprint because the underlying APIs were not yet built, I got reprimanded for unnecessarily blocking the build. My boss told me that I could build a front-end off of spec; the underlying infrastructure didn't need to be finished yet."

When we dig a little deeper, we discover that neither Rafael nor Tyson had a conversation with Gretchen about where or how this phantom UI was going to fit into the overall platform. They just logged their bits in Azure DevOps and moved on. At this revelation, I want to throw myself out of a second story window. I am frustrated that the teams can find the time to write pages and pages of user stories but cannot find ten minutes to sit down, face-to-face, and make sure they understand each other. We reset expectations: the UI will be connected to existing APIs. This project will re-skin the existing experience, not rebuild it. So, Gretchen and her team set off with this new direction in the following sprint.

Alignment Point C: end of the second sprint. In the sprint review, we see what is about to be released to production. We notice significant differences between the prototype in Rafael's DevOps feature and what is showcased in the sprint review. We ask Gretchen why the prototype for the new UI and what we were seeing look so different. Gretchen explains this is because they were limited by the project being a re-skin rather than a rebuild. Upon further investigation, we find that team Saturn, upon hearing the term re-skin, threw out the new application they had spent two weeks building prior to Alignment Point B.

They changed tactics and began updating the code in the existing UI for the purposes of re-skinning it. Well, as you can imagine, the product team is exasperated by this point, and the project has lost four weeks in wasted effort. After a lot of deep breaths and conversation, Rafael and Tyson realize that the miscommunication was down to Gretchen having a preconceived notion of the definition of the term re-skin. In her mind, the use of that term meant working on the existing source code base of the original UI.

However, that is not how Rafael meant the term. Rafael meant the new UI should connect to the existing APIs, and that the new application they had started to build was, in fact, the new skin. You can see why Gretchen would have interpreted the term as she did. But the fatal error here was not how Gretchen interpreted it or how Rafael used the term re-skin. The fatal error here is that they did not truly reach alignment. They didn't keep talking throughout the sprint. Gretchen did not communicate daily with Rafael to make sure her team was delivering what Rafael expected.

At all three alignment points, team members thought they were aligned. Their managers thought they were aligned. However, assumptions and different definitions of common terms prevented them from reaching true alignment. Misalignment was not identified quickly because the teams worked in silos, not alongside each other. Rafael, Tyson and Gretchen are only checking in with each other every two weeks.

Rafael should be speaking to Gretchen every day, especially after he realizes they have had a miscommunication. He should be speaking with her and her team about what they are coding, where they are coding it, and how it is going. Gretchen should reach out to Rafael when her team raises questions like: "Should this 'find my address' button connect to anything?" Rafael should have talked with Gretchen up front about using the existing APIs and asked Gretchen to explain how her team intended to tackle this project. Tyson should have worked with Gretchen and Corey to identify what data were available in the underlying APIs and aligned the prototype to the data available.

The players in the above example have not demonstrated a Generative type of corporate culture as described in Westrum's model. They are not oriented toward performance. Working software is not a consideration at the end of each sprint. They do not demonstrate high cooperation. The messenger, Gretchen, is not trained on how to guide her scrum to deliver on expectations. Risks are not shared. Multiple team members take a *not my problem* approach. Bridges across teams are weak – with stakeholders checking-in only at the end of each sprint. Failure leads to frustration and finger-pointing, not support and inquiry. Novelty is entirely ignored.

Blake puts his head in his hands. I reassure him this sort of thing happens more often than most teams want to admit (or realize). I say to him that we need to lay out the ground rules for communication, something that old people like us used to respect before communication was automated. I regularly kick my teams' asses to get out of their chairs and go talk to someone. Talk to a colleague. Talk to a customer. Stop writing emails like you are an Internet troll just because you think someone else made a mistake.

# How to Foster Open Communication
## Rule 1: Build Relationships

Effective communication relies on relationships. I could say the same thing to ten different people, and there would be ten different interpretations of what I meant based on my individual relationship with each person. Until you know someone well, you may hear what they say, but it is tough to know what they mean. Underlying personal relationships are important. People matter. Their motivations and emotional selves are critical parts of how they function in the workplace. Ignore this at your peril.

Many chunky corporates stop funding team-building exercises when financial performance plateaus. Ironically, when performance is struggling, you need teams to feel like teams more than ever. You may get away with skipping a few team days out, but, over time, you will undermine some of the core pillars of productivity. As colleagues become more distant from each other, the amount of trust they have in each other wanes. The credibility they afford each other declines. The likelihood they will give the other *the benefit of the doubt* in difficult circumstances falls to near zero.

Before you know it, in-fighting and blame-throwing are rife within the corporate culture. Weak relationships make us quick to blame others and slow to understand them. Teams become fractured and stop engaging with each other. Shared definitions of clear goals become cloudy. Strong relationships are critical to navigating missteps. When we understand our colleagues and our customers, we create safe environments where colleagues remain relentlessly and positively focused on delivering strong performance.

# Rule 2: Stop Typing; Start Talking

Effective communicators are comfortable having difficult conversations face-to-face. In the world of work, there will be days where the news is bad. Features will be delayed; performance will be less than perfect; we will make mistakes. Effective communicators and strong collaborators proactively share difficult messages with compassion and support, providing a safe space in which colleagues can be human. When something goes wrong, they reach out to affected stakeholders to let them know personally. Stakeholders should not have to chase for updates about critical bugs or other system issues. The journey to becoming a mature senior leader includes exercising this muscle. Effective leaders provide honest feedback when things are not going well. Leading by example is the best way to foster a culture of open, respectful communication regarding what is going well and what is not going well.

Bad news or negative feedback should never be delivered via electronic message. When communication gets tense, stop typing and start talking. Do not engage in electronic wars of words. They are no more effective in the workplace than they are on social media. If you have to tell a colleague or a customer that the feature they have been waiting for is delayed, if you have to tell a team member that his or her performance was below par, you must do that face-to-face. With the prevalence of video calling, there is absolutely no excuse for resorting to email to inform a colleague or customer of disappointing news.

Email may feel like the path of least resistance, but it pisses people off. Just stop doing it. Seriously. I don't care if you are Gen Z and you never learned to talk properly because you were WhatsApping before you could speak. Get your butt out of a seat and in front of a customer or colleague in actual proximity. Resolving conflict is more effective in person.

## Rule 3: Disagree Agreeably

Psychological safety is critical to fostering collaboration and cooperation. When teams start to fracture, one colleague will assume another colleague just generally makes bad decisions, has poor judgment, or never sees the big picture. In actual fact, that colleague has a different perspective from yours. And here's a hint: your perspective isn't perfect, either. You and your colleague will both benefit from sharing your perspectives and building a rich, diverse perspective that benefits from all of your collective knowledge.

Cross-functional teams can have productive debates about the best way to build a software feature. When they feel safe, people can be open and confident even when challenged by a colleague. When teams are defensive or feel threatened, perspective narrows. Promoting inclusive decision-making requires team members have the skills to diffuse tense situations, not escalate them. These are discrete skills that can be taught. Inclusive teams make better business decisions up to eighty-seven percent of the time,[2] according to research by Cloverpop.

The more inclusive the decision-making process, the better the decisions. This is the fundamental aim of fostering cross-functional collaboration. The finance team knows better than anyone what financial

---

[2] Larson, Erik. "New Research: Diversity + Inclusion = Better Decision Making At Work," September 21, 2017. www.forbes.com/sites/eriklarson/2017/09/21/new-research-diversity-inclusion-better-decision-making-at-work/?sh=62b6ccd44cbf.

software needs to deliver. The customer-facing team knows better than anyone what customers are trying to achieve. The technology team knows better than anyone what the software could do. Rely on your experts, regardless of team. These diverse points of view deserve consideration when building complex software. The more debate you have about a critical decision, the more likely you are to proactively identify and manage unintended consequences.

# Rule 4: Proactively Seek Alignment

Time is not on our side. This is what I hear over and over again from chunky corporate colleagues. Everyone feels overworked and under pressure to deliver against optimistic deadlines. Collaboration goes out the window when you feel you have more work than time. Seeking alignment with colleagues around complex decisions requires an investment. While we might all accept that investment of time will pay future dividends, it is hard to work that way when you are running late. If I am staring down a deadline to deliver a design document, or a feature, or anything else, I am less likely to seek alignment with my colleagues before delivering my work. They might slow me down! I can deliver the work faster if I just get my head down and get on with it. This is sound logic and hard to fault when it comes from an employee that just wants the project to go faster. However, it is a false economy. Working in a silo will result in poorer decision-making and carry unintended consequences in the future.

Proactive alignment is critical to avoiding the scenarios laid bare in this chapter. Teams must actively build bridges to reach alignment. Effective checkpoints at major design or build decisions require colleagues to collaborate with their cross-functional teams. It will help teams to identify any misalignment before features go into sprint and reduce inefficiencies in build. Seeking alignment means having difficult conversations with colleagues with whom you have a strong relationship, potentially engaging in productive debate, and getting to a place where you all agree on the best way to deliver on the business outcomes with which you are tasked. Delivering on rule four depends on mastering rules one to three.

## Key Takeaways

- Good execution depends on good communication.

- Proactively identifying and addressing assumptions will prevent feature re-work.

- Strong relationships deliver the best results.

# CHAPTER 12

# Driving Cross-Functional Collaboration

Let's fast forward a year from when Blake and Luke reported falling revenues and rising costs in Chapter 1. Every month, they have turned in figures that are behind budget. Every month they have said it will get better next month. The Board has lost patience. In an effort to build a decent story to tell the Board and prevent them freaking out, Blake hauls his team into a two-day offsite to get to the bottom of it.

Blake: "Anka, LaTonya, Tilen, we've talked through the high level numbers. Performance is faltering, and I am about to have my ass handed to me in the next Board meeting. What is going on?"

LaTonya: "Survey Division is losing customers to GS Survey, founded by Casey, our ex-colleague. Their product is not nearly as feature rich, but it is modern and fast."

Tilen: "Feedback from sales in the Publishing Division is that the rebuild of core applications has been painfully slow. We are losing existing customers and new deals to competitors. John, we have got to find a way to get the new applications delivered on time. Delays are killing us."

K. Tamblin, *The Lean-Agile Dilemma*, https://doi.org/10.1007/979-8-8688-0321-5_12

Anka: "New product launches in Analytics division have been lackluster. We thought the new ground based imagery product would plug the gaps in revenue, but it just isn't selling. There was a solid business case to back up the decision to take it forward. I think it is just taking longer than expected to get off the ground."

At this point, Blake wants to crawl into a small hole in the ground and hide. None of these issues have easy fixes. There is no panacea guaranteed to get a corporation this large and sophisticated back to peak performance in the sort of timeline that enables Blake to keep his job. He realizes that by the time poor product decisions impact financial performance numbers in a subscription business, the business is already way behind the curve.

Blake asks if I'll join him for a whiskey after day one of the offsite.

Blake: "I think this is bad. I'm starting to feel completely overwhelmed by the amount of issues we are facing in the different divisions. I can't go to the Board with this story. I'll be crucified."

Katie (*helpful as ever*): "Yep. Shit sandwich."

Blake: "We should have paid attention when customers like Joanne started to grumble. We should have invested in replatforming back then. We should have gotten the data and the design right before we started building the applications. Now, I wonder if we are too late."

Katie: "Well, we just have to pick ourselves up and right this ship. We can do it. We have a solid customer base, established products, and a right to win. Our biggest problem is that our people, particularly in product and technology, are spinning their wheels. They are spending time on tasks that simply aren't critical to delivering business goals. They need more focus and less distraction. We are overcomplicating everything. Let's simplify what we are asking the team to do."

Blake: "Totally. Sometimes I feel like the team makes building a pretty simple software platform sound as complicated as landing a rover on Mars. Let's get back to basics. What is our core value proposition? What software is required to deliver that to customers? What are we going to do, and who is going to do it?"

Chunky corporates are incredibly sophisticated systems. To maintain productivity growth well after an organization has achieved market maturity requires a bit of luck and a collaborative culture. Our chunky corporate is more like an organism than a machine: a complex amalgamation of systems that can work productively and efficiently or can break down and cause problems for each other. In highly mechanical businesses, hierarchical relationships between individuals can be effective. However, data- and technology-enabled businesses are not highly mechanical.

Building effective software depends upon creative thought and effective decision-making by a broad cast of colleagues. Colleagues who write code or make product decisions take input not just from their line managers, but from stakeholders across the business. They must have a deep understanding of what the business is trying to achieve to be successful. Based upon input from stakeholders, engineers apply individualized logic to writing lines of code. However, when we consider the managerial challenges of directing these colleagues to make decisions, we oversimplify these relationships. We think about colleagues in the context of an organizational chart, with engineers reporting into scrum masters, who report into a Head of Development, who reports into the Chief Technology Officer, who reports into the CEO. Acme's technology team is headed up by John, and his organization chart looks like Figure 12-1.

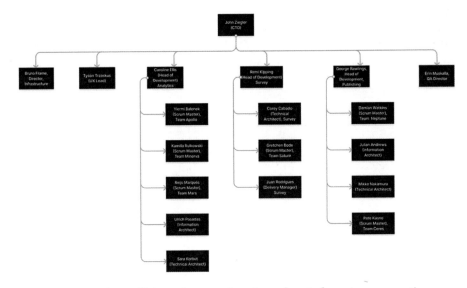

***Figure 12-1.*** *A traditional organization chart showing reporting lines of the technology team*

Meanwhile, product teams report up through divisional leadership, like Figure 12-2.

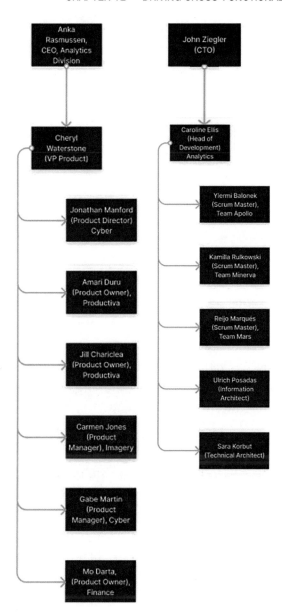

***Figure 12-2.*** *Product organization chart*

However, the relationships between the people that work in the organization look more like Figure 12-3.

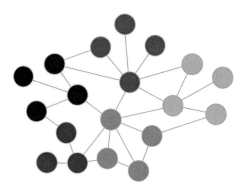

**Figure 12-3.** *Network organization diagram*

People do not interact with each other along hierarchical lines. People, especially in product management, work across the business. The strength of relationships colleagues have across teams is incredibly important. Yet, whenever we use an organization chart to describe the organization, we render these invisible. When we identify our organizations as complex systems, with thousands of relevant and useful relationships that underpin them, we start to see where critical stakeholders operate. Many leadership teams talk about stakeholder mapping and pay lip service to the indisputable fact that company culture influences performance. Many organizations carry out stakeholder mapping exercises, then put those maps on the shelf, never to be referenced again.

Colleagues don't automatically change the way they work off the back of being shown a stakeholder map at a singular point in time. Stakeholder maps should be continuous complements to the organization chart as part of daily business. Acme needs to implement a dual operating system,[1] as described by John P. Kotter, that enables cross-functional

---

[1] Kotter, John P. *Accelerate: Building Strategic Agility for a Faster-Moving World.* Harvard Business Review Press, 2014, p. 21.

collaboration alongside hierarchical management structures: "Populated with a diagonal slice of employees from all across the organization and up and down its ranks, the network liberates information from silos and hierarchical layers and enables it to flow with far greater freedom and at accelerated speed." Liberating a network isn't a management thing; it is something any product or technology colleague can do. The critical enabler of success in liberating the network is identifying the key stakeholders for each feature, epic, or project and recognizing they will change. Step one in embarking on building a piece of software is understanding who has the knowledge to define requirements, design a solution, and build it.

The network associated with any feature is fluid. Mapping relevant stakeholders identifies points of criticality. Stakeholders identified in a map help colleagues remember who needs to actively participate in the scoping and building of a software feature. So, what is it we are talking about documenting? In this context, we aim to understand the relationships between colleagues for the purposes of managing our product roadmap. A number of relationships are relevant to making sound product decisions. You will have direct reporting as shown in Figure 12-4.

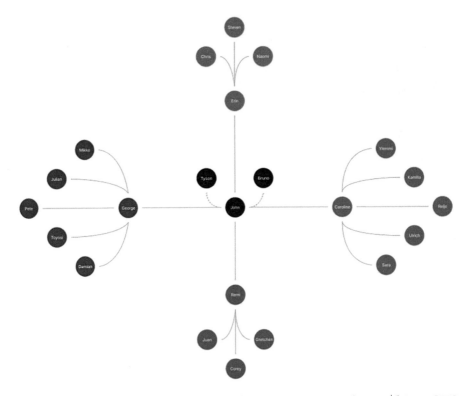

**Figure 12-4.** *Network diagram of direct reporting relationships, CTO*

Just as in the preceding hierarchy, we can see CTO, John, has six direct reports: Bruno, Director of Infrastructure; Tyson, UX Lead; Directors of Development (Caroline, George, and Remi); and a QA Director, Erin. We visualize these relationships and their direct reports modeled here in a network map, rather than a hierarchical organization chart. From here, we can overlay the relationships that these individuals have with other parts of the organization that fall outside of direct reporting lines. Product Owners in the technology team should have strong relationships with product managers across the regional divisions, who, in turn should have strong relationships with customer success, sales, marketing, and the back office functions the platform supports. When you map out these relationships, the network model gets more complex, and you start to see that product functions have a high connectivity to the rest of the organization.

In Figure 12-5, we look at the significant relationships between Lev, the VP of Product, Survey Division, and key stakeholders working on enhancements to the Survey platform, for the purposes of remaining competitive with GS Tech.

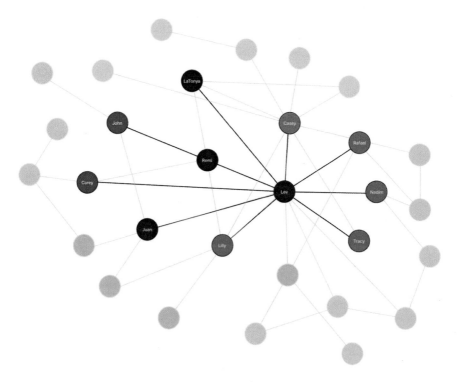

**Figure 12-5.** *Network diagram of influencing relationships, VP of Product, Survey Division*

Three product owners and a product director report to Lev, who reports to the Regional CEO, LaTonya, and has a strong relationship with the CTO, John. Lev also has strong relationships with technology team members who report up through the technology Division of Acme: Remi,

Head of Development; Juan, Delivery Manager; and Corey, Technical Architect. Lev would have a very strong relationship with the VP of Sales in Survey Division, Casey, but he has left the business. You can see there are many more relationships in this system map of people, but for the purposes of simplicity, we are highlighting the most important in the context of this particular workstream. This exercise also helps us to understand with whom Lev should liaise in sales, given Casey's departure from the business. By following the relationships to Casey's position, LaTonya can quickly determine who are the critical people for Lev to engage with in Casey's absence, until his position is filled.

Lev should consult or inform these key stakeholders throughout the software build that impacts them. If the timelines change, these stakeholders should be told. If there are questions about how to achieve business outcomes, these stakeholders should be consulted. If the scope changes, these stakeholders should be active participants in the discussion. Some stakeholder maps will remain relatively stable over time. Other stakeholder maps may be relevant to a particular software epic. They also don't always have to look the same.

In the figure below, we highlight an example created to document stakeholders relevant to a particular feature enhancement. If you recall, in Chapter 2, Ella and Jamie struggled to get aligned around development of the essay review feature. Jamie had expectations regarding future enhancements that couldn't easily be accommodated by the feature. Their lack of communication meant additional work could have been avoided if Ella and Jamie were clear up front about the context of the feature and future expectations of its functionality. Ella, Pete, and Julian also struggled to achieve an efficient, clear design regarding reference data in the platform. Their miscommunications resulted from conversations between Julian, Pete, and Ella taking place after Pete's team had started coding the feature, rather than in the design phase. They discussed what Ella needed from the feature after the MVP was built, which was too late. However, if Roberta and George, the line managers for these respective teams, made it mission critical that designs and requirements must result out of close collaboration between the stakeholders in Figure 12-6, these sorts of inefficiencies could have been minimized.

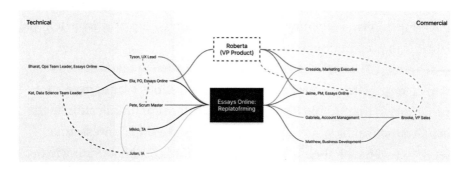

**Figure 12-6.** *Stakeholder mapping, replatforming project, Essays Online*

George: "Julian, I like the changes you made to the data design. They seem simpler and cleaner. Have you run them by Ella to ensure there are no unintended consequences?"

Julian: "No, I haven't had a chance. Ella has been super busy working with Jamie on requirements for the next feature to go in sprint. I can't get in her diary."

George: "Forget diary scrambling. Just drop her a Slack message and give her a call. This isn't signed off until you've walked her through it. And, I mean *walk her through it*…dropping data designs in her inbox and assuming if you don't hear from her that she has no objections is not good enough. Got me? If you can't get time with her today, let me know. I'll speak to Roberta to work on helping Ella to free up the time."

Julian: "Yes, I got it."

The effectiveness of collaboration across stakeholders determines the effectiveness of the end product. In time, as Roberta and George continue to bang this drum, their teams will realize features do not move into sprint until stakeholders have been consulted. Collaboration with stakeholders in the diagram becomes part of doing business. This is the critical element that chunky corporates should take from Agile principles and adapt to their more sophisticated networks. The scrum team assigned to a feature codes it, but they should not code it in a vacuum. Cross-functional communication among identified stakeholders for the purposes of delivering a software feature should be considered top priority when that feature is in preparation or in sprint.

If a squad of stakeholders assigned to a particular feature needs to meet to agree to the design or to answer questions as they come up during sprint, that should be the most important communication of the day. These stakeholders should be empowered to skip non-essential meetings (even with their line managers) in favor of collaborating in the squad. This is particularly true for the non-scrum members of the squad. Their priority is to keep the scrum working. If members of the scrum have unanswered questions, they will either make poorly informed decisions or they will pause coding altogether until their questions are answered. Both outcomes are inefficient.

Chunky corporates often have so many developers that technical architects and quality-assurance resources are specialists who no longer form part of the scrum. In contrast, on a small team, a technical architect would spend half her time coding and half her time designing. At larger organizations, it is more likely that a technical architect would spend all of her time working on technical designs across a range of features coded by different scrum teams. This has positive and negative implications. It helps the teams to maintain consistent designs, but it means that the architects are not imbedded in the scrum in the way they would traditionally have been.

Chunky corporates need to adjust for this by making *squads,* teams that include the scrum, but also the product owner, technical architect, information architect, data scientist, quality assurance, and any relevant business stakeholders. Engineers would only ever be in one scrum, but an architect, data scientist, product manager, or business partner may be in multiple squads. Stakeholder mapping of the squads working concurrently at any given time will highlight if resources are stretched too thin. If specialists are expected to support multiple scrums, they must be managed carefully to avoid bottlenecks.

When we document the relationships product leaders have across an organization, we find they are more plentiful, and span a much larger group than many other job functions. It's why product leaders spend most of their time talking to people. Driving productivity means spending that time wisely. Product owners and product managers sit at the intersection of a lot of stakeholders, and their calendars can be overrun with meetings very quickly if this is not managed. In nerdy math terms, we say that product owners have a greater *centrality* to the system than other players. Centrality, in the context of network data, measures the importance of an entity based on its relationships to other entities.

In laypersons terms, what the above picture tells you is that product owners and product managers are at the center of feature delivery. They should maintain strong relationships with members of the technology team, members of the product team, and members of sales, marketing, and customer support teams. When working on features that serve internal customers, they should build strong relationships with the internal business partners with appropriate expertise: finance for invoicing features, operations for process-enabling features, sales for CRM integration. Product managers and product owners facilitate the flow of information horizontally across hierarchical silos. These relationships are critical to the success of software development, and yet, because they cut across reporting lines, are rarely managed explicitly. Or, put colloquially, product people have all the responsibility with none of the control. They have to be extremely effective influencers to balance tensions across stakeholders, none of whom report into them in the organizational hierarchy.

Teams should leverage stakeholder mappings like the above, laid out in link graphs, enabling them to visualize the people critical to delivery of various projects or individual software features.

# Keys to Successful Usage of Stakeholder Maps

1.  Responsibility and accountability are clearly defined for each stakeholder.

2.  Priority of communication is in the workstream over general or unrelated meetings.

3.  Fluidity of stakeholder maps is accepted, and stakeholder groups change with each epic.

When you map workstreams in the above fashion, the critical members of your team as they relate to the delivery of key business goals will jump off the page. They are the ones with the most relationships. If you are in the midst of a replatforming project, they are also probably drowning in work and making hasty decisions as a result. This type of mapping yields a decidedly different point of view as compared to your typical org chart. Often, the most critical characters associated with delivering a successful replatforming exercise are not on the radar of the investor/owners of the business. It sounds absurd when you put it bluntly, but the people who will determine the success or failure of your replatforming exercise are probably invisible to your senior leadership team. They are not at the top of the org chart. They are the ones in the middle. They are the ones most central to facilitating cross-functional collaboration.

# Key Takeaways

-   Deep involvement of cross-functional stakeholders drives efficiency.

-   Teams should prioritize the stakeholder network over the hierarchy to relentlessly deliver working features.

-   Understanding the centrality of stakeholders can highlight potential project bottlenecks.

# CHAPTER 13

# Final Thoughts

So, you've read these pages and realized that much of what is written here sounds familiar. Hooray! You are now part of a large community of organizations facing similar struggles. Lean-Agile software development principles were not written with chunky corporates in mind. The application of these principles to software development at large, mature software businesses breeds tension and frustration, not radical success. However, if we adapt these principles to the constraints chunky corporates face, we can unlock previously inaccessible productivity. We can deliver on the business outcomes that product and technology resources were hired to deliver.

## Acknowledge Your Constraints

Set yourself apart by recognizing your software projects are constrained to set milestones, fixed budgets, and predetermined timelines. For investor/ owners, predictable performance beats innovation. Risk is margin-diluting. Launching any new product is risky. It diverts attention from the existing product stack and requires up-front investment with unproven returns. External investors from the private equity, financial, or public realm have a much lower tolerance for risk than venture capitalists.

Ensure everyone at your organization knows these constraints, too. Be crystal clear with your product and technology teams: you are not looking for wild innovation or exciting new features that lack guaranteed financial returns. Focus on delivering predictable financial performance through strict execution against defined goals. Be honest about what you want: it isn't sexy, no, but it is stable and steady, which is what most colleagues need over the long term, even if they don't realize it.

# Get Comfortable Saying No

You will have noticed I use the word *focus* a lot throughout this book. Lack of focus is at the heart of many chunky corporate missteps. People don't mean to lose focus. The most common cause is an inability to set appropriate boundaries: a customer who wants a new button; a salesperson who can close a deal if we add a feature; and a marketeer convinced the company can capture explosive growth if we add a new product.

Scope of development requested is greater than capacity to deliver it. The most efficient corporations have ruthless stage gates that determine on which features it is worth spending precious development resources. The earlier you say no, the less resource you waste chasing a dream your investors have no intention of making reality.

# Replatform the Right Way

If you are a chunky corporate, most of your time will be spent rebuilding existing products. Rather than innovating and iterating in pursuit of an unproven user base, relentlessly deliver agreed milestones aligned to a defined vision. Define your waypoints with senior leadership and key stakeholders across the business. Learn from your history and spend more time than your lean counterparts on design of a platform that does what the old one did, just better and faster. Stop confusing your teams by pursuing a replatforming project according to Lean-Agile principles. Adopt an Orienteering methodology for developing software and prioritize execution.

# Remember the Data

Build your house on good foundations. When replacing or merging software platforms, organize your data first. Data are the skeleton off of which software applications hang, not the other way around. We are in the Information Age; you cannot leave your fortune to something the technology team sees as a byproduct of building applications. If you do not manage data proactively, any value you get from data will be by chance.

Flow existing data into the database (or warehouse, data lake, or knowledge graph) before starting to code. The efficiency of your code will depend on how successfully you minimize data surprises over the life of your replatforming project. Get the data right first, and write the code after.

# Build a Flexible, Scalable Product Stack

Ensure that your data, product, and technology teams are tightly aligned around building a product stack that can pivot and scale without code adjustments. Drill the team regularly on the product-package-subscription definition in your platform. Define a clear objective for all players in the team to build products in this way. Design test cases that check multiple future combinations of users, features, products, packages, and subscriptions.

A flexible product stack will maximize your organization's ability to align revenue to customer value. The more flexibly you can combine features into products and products into packages, the more ably you can charge your customers the maximum they are willing to pay for the features that matter to them. And it comes with an added benefit: if this part of your platform is flexible, you can confidently minimize future rework. You can introduce additional product layers, or adjust products based on market evolution, without requiring significant code changes.

# Recognize the Strengths and Weaknesses of Being a Complex System

Acknowledge that your chunky corporate is a sophisticated system of stakeholders. Map out cross-functional teams and identify important relationships that sit outside of the corporate hierarchy. Hold teams accountable for achieving effective collaboration.

When your team is collaborating cross-functionally, you can achieve amazing things. Foster transparent, honest, assertive, and respectful collaboration among team members at all levels of the organization. Respect the expertise of specialist roles and empower those specialists to deliver excellent products by balancing their priorities effectively. Embrace your complexity and leverage it to your advantage.

**Two years later:**

Blake: "How did you find that last Board meeting?"

Katie: "What a difference a year makes, eh?"

Blake: "Too right."

Katie: "It is fantastic to see the green shoots of growth returning to the business."

Blake: "Indeed. You can feel it across the organization. I know it is only one quarter of growth so far, but I'm really confident we are back on the right path. No doubt it will come in fits and starts, but we've put the right things in place to continue improving."

Katie: "How is the replatforming coming along?"

Blake: "Survey Division? Much better. We've put in place a lot of changes based on past lessons learned. We have data coming from the legacy platform via a regular feed into the new database, which is a solid foundation on which to build new code. While we weren't thrilled to pause coding for the three months it took to get that data foundation in place, it is accelerating our migration timeline. Customers are logging in to the new UI already to see how their data looks and to help us prepare for future migrations."

Katie: "And John's team? How are tech releases coming along?"

Blake: "Night and day. I had no idea how much time they were wasting responding to and evaluating requests for features that we shouldn't be building. I've made it very clear, throughout the organization, that we will be laser-focused on delivering the software features already defined. Any exceptions go through a rigorous evaluation process, and the teams making the decisions feed that back to all stakeholders. Any time we have to pivot and add a previously unexpected feature to the road map, we choose another feature of similar size to drop or postpone. That, also, is fed back to stakeholders and customers. This has massively boosted our confidence in software delivery."

Katie: "I think the first time I ever used the term chunky corporate, you winced."

Blake: "Probably."

Katie: "And now?"

Blake: "Now I appreciate it isn't an insult. Being big comes with challenges but also huge benefits. Yes, we have to work harder to collaborate well, but we can offer a level of stability and predictability that lean startups can't match. It's like a Renaissance painting you know? Back then, a bigger size meant you were rich enough to eat well."

Katie: "In the corporate world, it still does."

# Index

© Katie Tamblin 2024
K. Tamblin, *The Lean-Agile Dilemma*, https://doi.org/10.1007/979-8-8688-0321-5

Printed in the United States
by Baker & Taylor Publisher Services